"We gravitate toward stories because, like a map and compass, they direct us back home — home to an inspired heart. Rivvy's stories will take you there ... and with a few miracles in your pocket."

> — BRIAN LUKE SEAWARD, Ph.D.,
> author of *Stand Like Mountain, Flow Like Water*

"Morsels of experience served up with Rivvy's special blend of wry wit and a warm heart. Each time I dip into her stories, I remember that living itself is delicious!"

> — PRISCILLA STUCKEY, author of *Kissed by a Fox: And Other Stories of Friendship in Nature*

"Clear. Profound. Homey. This is the *Eat, Pray, Love* of everyday life!"

> — MARILYN WEBB, Pulitzer Prize-nominated author of *The Good Death*, and former Editor-in-Chief of *Psychology Today*

"I really love this book! It charms and inspires. What more could one ask?"

> — HAL ZINA BENNETT, author of *Write from the Heart: Unleashing the Power of Your Creativity*

"It's smart, funny, and moving. It invites in the believers and welcomes the skeptics. And reading it made me feel great!"

> — BARBARA FISHER, book critic and correspondent for the *Boston Globe*

"Rivvy's delightful stories open the heart. Read them, one at a time, and then daydream on them ... and you will take on a glow of joy and feel more secure in God's world."

— RABBI ZALMAN SCHACHTER-SHALOMI, author of
Davening: A Guide to Meaningful Jewish Prayer

"A reflective, joyful journey that will likely change the way you see the world."

— MATTHEW BARBER, Tony-nominated
playwright of *Enchanted April*

"This is a wise and wonderful book of recipes to help cook up a more delicious life!"

— ALLY SHEEDY, film and stage actress and
author of *Yesterday I Saw the Sun: Poems*

"Rivvy Neshama is a wonderful storyteller, and her book is filled with memorable tales. There is sweetness and light here, and a guide to thoughtful ways to enhance those daily miracles of life that connect us to our better selves, and to others."

— JAY NEUGEBOREN, author of *The American Sun &
Wind Moving Picture Company* and *You Are My Heart*

"I love *Recipes for a Sacred Life* and you will too. The stories are inspiring, enlightening, and entertaining. Everyone should read this book. Sit back and enjoy!"

— DHARMA SINGH KHALSA, M.D., author of *The
New Golden Rules* and co-author of *Meditation As
Medicine*

Rivvy Neshama

RECIPES FOR
A SACRED LIFE

TRUE STORIES
and a few miracles

DIVINE
ARTS

Published by DIVINE ARTS
DivineArtsMedia.com

An imprint of Michael Wiese Productions
12400 Ventura Blvd. # 1111
Studio City, CA 91604
(818) 379-8799, (818) 986-3408 (Fax)

Cover Design: JohnnyInk www.johnnyink.com
Interior Design: John Brenner and Jay Anning
Copy Editor: Matt Barber

Printed by McNaughton & Gunn, Inc., Saline, Michigan
Manufactured in the United States of America

Library of Congress Cataloging-in-Publication Data
Neshama, Rivvy.
 Recipes for a sacred life : true stories and a few miracles / Rivvy Neshama.
   pages cm
 Includes bibliographical references.
 ISBN 978-1-61125-020-6
1. Spiritual life. 2. Spirituality. I. Title.
 BL624.N475 2013
 204'.4--dc23
                                2013015969

Printed on Recycled Stock

DEDICATION

*To my mother, Irene Dashevsky Feldman, inspiration,
dearest friend, and Princess of Germantown Ave,
with whom this all began*

*To my father, Bernard Saul Feldman, a teller of tales and a
lover of life, with a spirit so big he still speaks in this book*

*To my son, Tony, and daughter, Elise, for the love,
the lessons, and the journey together*

*To my grandchildren, Brendan, Jenna, Eli, Isaac, and Jordan,
for the joy they give so abundantly (for which I am
grateful to their loving parents!)*

And to John, my beloved. Of course.

TABLE OF CONTENTS

Part Three
ANIMAL CHATS AND
OTHER UNIONS WITH NATURE

Part Four
TO FORGIVE IS DIVINE

Part Five
FRIENDS AND NEIGHBORS,
LOVERS AND STRANGERS

LA COCINERA (THE COOK)

These teachings,
take them with a grain of salt,
the salt of your own being,
your own mind and heart.

Sniff it out.
Does it smell right?
Eso no, esta si.
This yes, that no.

Don't be afraid to pick
and choose.
That's what cooks do
when they are making a dish.
Este plato es tu propio mismo.
This dish is you!

— ELLEN STARK, 2009

BEGINNINGS

I'm not much of a cook. Neither was my mother. And that's how it all began. When I was twenty-two and about to get married, she gave me a recipe book, the kind with blank pages to write down or paste in all your best recipes. Mom had written down hers to get things started, but she only had two: roast beef and chicken. Like I said, she wasn't much of a cook. Still, she made a great roast, and here were her notes on just how to do it: "*Set oven at 450. Season roast with salt and garlic. Sear for 30 min., lower temp to 350, cook for 1 hour.*"

That was it. Nice and simple. The chicken recipe was pretty much the same.

So I got married, made roast beef and chicken, and if a friend ever cooked something tasty, I found out how and wrote it down in the book.

It was several pages in and one month later that I found more notes from Mom: *"Wash your delicates with Ivory Snow in cold water."* That's no recipe, I thought. Then I thought, Why not? Mom was passing on whatever she hoped would prepare me for a good marriage, a good life.

Well, both marriage and life turned out to be much harder than I ever imagined. I didn't know that after eight years and two children I'd be getting divorced. Or that the existential angst that looked so cool in French movies would be painful, not fun. Or that moments of great happiness and meaning could be swallowed by moments of fear. I didn't know that outside of movies and books, this was life, and I often wished I had recipes telling me what to do, how to live, which path to take.

Meanwhile, my own path became one of exploring: a little this, a little that, whatever seemed to work. It could be whatever lowered the pain or anxiety I sometimes found in living, or whatever brought the greatest joy and lifted me to a higher level. I studied yoga and meditation, tried therapy and drugs, went to rallies and retreats. And my spiritual path became a smorgasbord that merged Eastern and Western religions, Native traditions, and my mom.

I also, over time, grew up, met and married my beloved John, and moved to the foothills of Boulder, Colorado.

It was many years later — after my children were married, after I'd sat and held hands with a friend who was dying, and after my highs and lows had somewhat smoothed out — that I saw an intriguing exercise in a book. It was titled "Find Your Highest Purpose." Now, I'm a real patsy for these kinds of quizzes. They're the esoteric version of the "What Kind of Guy Is Right for You?" quizzes I took endlessly as a teen. So I closed my eyes as the book suggested, recalled three times when I felt passionate about something I did, looked for the common threads — the essence of my passion — opened my eyes and wrote down "My highest purpose is ...." And something inside me let me fill in the rest: "...to live a sacred life." *Well that was a surprise.* But then I wrote more, as I imagined what it would look like and how it would feel:

A simple life, filled with love, awe, and a deep sense of connection. A happy life, touched with grace and blessings. A life in which I know what I'm here to do — and do it.

And finally, as the book directed, I summed it all up in a way I'd remember:

My highest purpose is to live a sacred life, connected to others, nature, and the divine through love, gratefulness, and service.

It wasn't long after I did this that I got a call from Carol, the editor of a magazine I sometimes wrote for. She asked me if I'd write an article on creating a sacred space in your home. Well, sure, I said, hearing the drumroll of synchronicity.

My research began with friends who had shrines or meditation rooms, and ended with a Native American Feng Shui master who happened to live nearby. We sat by a fountain in her living room — painted the colors of earth and sky and enriched with carvings of wood and stone — while she spoke about the power of color and the four elements and how they can bring magic and nature into your house and your life.

Her words touched me, and so did her home. Walking back to my street, I felt lighter, in a way I remembered but hadn't been for some time. I began to write the article in my head — "How to Create a Sacred Space" — when suddenly, I had an inspiration, a nudge from above: Rivvy, write a *book* — How to Create a Sacred LIFE! Of course, I responded. Will do. And it was soon after then that I began to remember and encounter the people and experiences that make up this book.

That's how it works. The first step toward any goal is setting the intention; it's your prayer and personal GPS.

I remember being startled the first time my son's car spoke. Tony entered his destination and *presto*! This strange but knowing voice told him how to reach it. "Turn left at the light and go straight for three miles...." If I needed more proof, this was it: Let the universe know your intention, and you'll be guided all the way there.

Why me? Why you?
And you don't have to be perfect to live sacred.

Why me? Well, my English friend Helen, who served faithfully as my first reader, seemed to nail it. She stopped by one day when I was in a Jewish mood, worrying about everything I could think of, from getting a new bed to dying. "Rivvy," Helen said, "read your book!" Then she added, with blunt British humor, "If anyone needs to be writing this, it's you!"

Why you? Why not? Life is sacred — for everyone, not just monks and mystics. But to feel it and see it, there are things you can do, things that bring out the wonder and connectedness of everything in life. It begins with your intention, looking in. And it's furthered by your attention, looking out.

One of the gurus I went to hear in the seventies was a man known simply as Stephen, who started a commune known as The Farm. His teaching I remember most was this: Attention is energy. What you put your attention into, you get more of. He meant it literally, too, giving a whole new meaning to "What you see is what you get." At the same time, attention requires openness: open eyes, open mind. Being open to the sacred allows you to recognize it when it appears. And finally, attention means *pay* attention. On Rosh Hashanah, the Jewish New Year, a ram's horn called the shofar is blown for all to hear. Its piercing sound is meant to wake us up — to life, to who we are, to how we want to be.

And so, with intention and attention, I started writing this book. And the more I wrote, the more recipes I found, and the happier and more radiant my life and I became. What I didn't become was much of a cook. Like Mom, I'm the roast-a-chicken type, and the recipes I've written are that simple, with most of them passed on through stories.

So here they are.
So here they are, my recipes for a sacred life: some from family and friends, some from teachers and writers, some made up along the way ... but all tested, tried, and true. They lift me up when I'm feeling down, help me look out when I'm focused within, and lead me back to my center, the moment, and the joy of a sacred life.

I'm sure there are many here that you already know and just needed to be reminded of (writing them down helped remind me). Some are old-fashioned things your parents did or you once did and then forgot about. Some will seem just right; others you might not like at all, and that's okay (if you don't like fish, don't make fish for dinner). But what I hope is this: that you find a few that will add to the wonder, love, and sacredness of your life. Those are the ones to follow. Those are the ones to keep.

Part One

BASIC
INGREDIENTS

*"It's the basics, the footwork,
the where to begin ..."*

A GOOD DAY TO DIE...
OR *NOT*

Our culture is not too keen about death and dying. Truth is, neither am I. Perhaps I'd be more open if we could end our days by just fading into the night — after a great dinner with folks we love. I also find death much more acceptable on days when I'm feeling immortal than on days when I'm wondering, with anxiety, why I still have that peculiar pain.

This lapse of faith leads me to read many books about the cycles of life and death. Then I study other cultures that seem to have a deeper awareness of this sacred circle, like the Native Americans. When Chief Crazy Horse went into battle, he proclaimed, "It's a good day to die!" Some American Indians still say it, every day, to be ready for death and to live their best life.

So I started saying it myself in my morning salutations, after blessing the day and the world. And when I open my arms wide and look out at the sky and mountains, I often feel it: It *is* a good day. A good day to die. To merge with the universe and see what comes next. I especially feel it on blue-sky days when the crows are squawking and the trees are in bloom. Yes, I think, if I have to die, this would be a good day for it. (Notice I'm still using the "if"?)

Then, one morning, while my eighty-something mother was visiting from Philadelphia, she came out on the patio and sat down nearby, just as I was doing my morning "hellos" to the sun, birds, et al. She regards my diverse spiritual practices with some bemusement, but tries not to intrude when I'm at it. Still, she's also curious, which spurred her to move closer to hear.

"Hello to the birds and the deer," I said, arms open wide.

"Don't forget the squirrels," Mom interrupted.

"Hello to the flowers, bushes, and trees."

"You have some beautiful trees," Mom said. "Really."

Finally, I spread my arms even wider and announced, "It's a good day to die!"

"Well," Mom chirped in, "it's not a bad day to live either."

She had a point. So now I end my blessings like this:

"It's a good day to die!" I say.

And then, with gusto, "It's a good day to live!"

THE WHERE TO BEGIN

Deepak Chopra is known for his many books of guidance. The one I like best and keep at my bedside is *The
Seven Spiritual Laws of Success.* It's a small book with short
chapters in which he tells it like it is: Do this and you'll
get that. And if you follow his advice, what you'll get is:
"Harmony with nature," "Success in every endeavor,"
and "An experience of the miraculous." Not bad.

In Chapter One, Chopra presents the first law, the
"Law of Pure Potentiality." Here, he shows us how to
create the openness that can lead to fulfillment. It's a
simple recipe — only four things to do daily — and when
I first read it, it seemed easy:

1. Have a time of silence and stillness when you do
   nothing at all. (Sounds good!)
2. Meditate. (Check!)
3. Spend some time in nature — say, watching the
   moon rise — and feel the beauty and perfection
   of the universe. (Got it!)
4. Practice non-judgment throughout the day, beginning with an intention like, "Today, I will not
   judge." (Right!)

Ready to go, I began meditating on a daily basis, even
if only for five minutes. I also remembered to sit still a

bit and not even read. Then I'd walk outside to stare at a flower or the sky. And finally, I began to notice when I would judge.

What I noticed was I judge almost *always,* and I didn't know how to stop. I judge myself, I judge others, I judge myself for judging others. I judge friends, strangers, events. I judge neighbors, politicians, the weather … I'm an all-inclusive judge!

This was not good news. I wanted to move on to the second law, and the third, and fourth … and live a life of Harmony, Success, and Miracles. But I felt I couldn't read further until I had the first law down cold. Otherwise, it would feel like cheating. Besides, it probably wouldn't work.

So I kept rereading Chapter One. Then I would meditate, be silent, look at the birds … and watch myself judge. It was hopeless, and so was I.

It reminded me of the salsa class John and I took one winter. Our teacher, Carmen, made the lessons so easy that within a few weeks we were moving our hips, getting the rhythm, and feeling, hey, we can do this. But in the last two sessions, Carmen taught turns, and try as we would, this was not meant to be. John would turn one way, I would turn the other, and we'd never end up in the same place at the same time.

The next month, Carmen offered Level 2 classes; but knowing our problem with turns, we signed up for another go at Level 1. This worked out well. We got even better at the basics. So good, in fact, that Carmen said, "Watch John and Rivvy," and made us dance at the front of the room. Our classmates were impressed with our style and savvy — until session five, when Carmen again taught turns. Well, I thought, we could just keep signing up for Level I and have a few weeks of glory.

With that same reasoning, I decided I could make Deepak's first law my life's practice. And then, one day, while yet again reading Chapter One, I noticed something he wrote that I must have skimmed over before. If a whole day of non-judging seems too daunting, he said, start smaller. Say something like, "For the next two hours, I won't judge at all." Or lower the bar even more: "Just this hour, I will not judge."

This sounded doable, and indeed, I could do it! For one hour, I would notice whenever I was judging, let it go, and move on. And as I stopped judging, I began to feel a wonderful lightness, a sense that everything, including myself, was okay.

At last, I was ready to move on to Chapter Two, "The Law of Giving," and step up my spiritual life. But the funny thing is, I'm still reading Chapter One, over and over, and practicing the "Law of Pure Potentiality." It's the basics, the footwork, the where to begin — just like Carmen's first class got us out there and dancing.

GRATEFUL IN HARLEM

I don't always feel that grateful. Sometimes, when things are really bad, I don't even try. But then I remember the darkest time of my life, and meeting Billie, and learning the power of being grateful.

My first marriage, to the man I thought was my soul mate, had ended. We parted, he found a new place, and our two young children, Tony and Elise, moved back and forth between us, clutching their overnight bags and looking as confused and fragile as we were.

It wasn't long after then that I began to have panic attacks. I didn't know that's what they were called. I only knew I couldn't breathe and thought I was dying or going crazy. Night after night, I sat up in bed, praying for sleep or to make it through.

Most of all, I prayed for salvation. And it came through two things: my job and my children. They made me get up and keep moving; they gave me a purpose and a life.

The job was in Harlem. I was a community organizer helping school kids at risk. A team of us worked out of a church, and we were a motley crew: one ex-debutante, two guys from the 'hood, one church lady, and me — white girl with good intentions.

The men were a lively pair, always slapping each other and giving high fives. They seemed to bop more than walk, and their talk was fast and fluid. But what I liked most about them was they were real — no fake smiles, no pretense at all — and I found that comforting. They didn't hide their pain: I saw it in their faces. I even saw it sometimes in the face of our boss, the activist reverend Dr. C. I once asked Dr. C how he was doing and he said, "I'm hangin' in, honey, hangin' in by a thread."

The one who helped hold us up was the church lady, Billie, a handsome, hearty black woman whose humor was sharp but softened by her smile. She was my first live church lady, full of faith, and her own calm center helped me feel anchored and safe. And then there were her cakes, baked from scratch, awesome cakes with lemon icing that she'd bring to the church.

One day Billie found me crying and asked, "What's wrong, child?" What's wrong seemed beyond words. I was lost, frightened, and deeply depressed. With my soul mate gone, I forgot who I was, and each day was a battle against my own pain.

What made the pain worse was that it felt unworthy, compared to what I saw daily in Harlem: junkies falling in slow motion on sidewalks, and young kids killing themselves or others.

"Your pain is your pain," Billie said softly. "We've all got our struggle. But what *you* need, child, is to practice some gratefulness." Then she gave me this recipe to help me begin.

Billie told me to get a journal and write down each night — free form, no thinking — two lists, as long as I could make them. One was to be titled "I'm grat f for …," and the second was "I love in me…."

"Just write down whatever comes to mind," Billie said, "and they can be the same things each time."

So that's what I did nightly, before trying to sleep. Sometimes my two lists would merge: *"I'm grateful for* ... the walk I took in the park" and *"I love in me* ... walking in the park." The more I did it, the more things came to mind:

"I'm grateful for ... my children ... eating soul food at Sylvia's...."

"I love in me ... my smile ... teaching Lakisha to read...."

Just writing these lists, I began to feel better; each line was a rope that pulled me to shore.

But there's more to this story. For there still were days lost to despair, when I felt too broken to ever feel grateful. On one of those days, a cold day in November, I left work, trudged through soot and snow to the subway, and walked slowly, very slowly, down to the train. It was impossible to move any faster because of the three elderly women in front of me, who cautiously stepped down the wet, slushy stairs.

It's hard for me to tell the ages of older black women. They don't wrinkle and dry up like white people do. But I could see that they were very old, these women, with their hollowed cheeks and white wispy hair. And I could tell how poor they were by the thin, worn-out coats they wore in this, the coldest of winters.

One of the women, the eldest perhaps, would rest on her cane and speak after each step. She was instantly echoed by her two friends, as if they were her congregation.

"Praise the Lord!" she commanded.

"Praise the Lord!" they repeated.

Slowly, carefully, another step was taken.

"God is *good* to us!" she said with reverence.

"God is *good* to us!" they acknowledged.

All three now leaned on their canes or the railing, tired, out of breath, in old-age pain. And while they rested, I wondered about their prayer. God is good to us? They thought that now? Shivering in their thin coats, barely able to move?

Then their leader took another step, looked upward and said, "It could be worse!"

Suddenly turning to face me, she asked, "Right, missy? It could be worse?"

She stumbled, almost losing her balance, so I offered my arm.

"Yes, ma'am, " I agreed, as we walked down together. "It could be worse."

Which is why, years later, I still write my gratefuls. On good days, they're a way to always give thanks. And on bad days, each line helps to pull me to shore — and reminds me, it could be worse.

. . . .

"Life is glorious, but life is also wretched. It is both.
Gloriousness and wretchedness need each other.
One inspires us; the other softens us. They go together."
— PEMA CHÖDRÖN

TEA AND COMPASSION

While staying in Manhattan to visit family, I went with
John one Sunday to see my Sufi teacher, Halil Baba. He
had asked us to meet him at Aisha's apartment, where
we'd all met twice before. The first time it had felt
strange, seeing him in a mundane setting and wearing a
sweater and pants, instead of the white robe and prayer
cap he wore as a sheikh. But his kind, weathered face and
soft brown eyes were familiar, and it was a special treat
to be together at Aisha's. Nonetheless, on this day I felt
uneasy because John and I had just had a fight.

I have a dark side. I guess all people do. But mine just
might be a little darker. Anyway, most people don't get to
see that part of me. I save it for my dearest John — a dubious
honor. Not that John is perfect. Still, like most men, his
sins are more passive — grumpiness, sins of omission —
while mine have drama and flair. I won't go into scary
details, but I've noticed that when I'm bad, I'm often bad
the same way. Later, I feel so remorseful, and John always
forgives me, though I have trouble forgiving myself. I also
feel like a total phony if I'm off to do something spiritual,
like writing this book or hanging out with Halil Baba.

Which is why I felt uneasy that Sunday afternoon
when John and I went to Aisha's to meet him, right after
one of my darker moments. If he knew what I'm *really*
like, I thought, he wouldn't want to be my teacher.

Aisha, a fellow Sufi, lives on the Upper East Side and, like Halil Baba, is from Turkey, where hospitality must be a national trait. She always welcomes us so graciously: "John! Rabia!" she exclaims with great pleasure, Rabia being my Sufi name. And no matter what time it is, she offers us an abundance of Turkish delights — vine leaves stuffed with rice and nuts, carrots in olive oil, sweet chocolate halva — which she serves on a round brass tray. With Halil Baba, we sit in a circle on the floor, resting on large velvet pillows as we eat, sip tea, and exchange niceties.

No one does niceties like the Sufis from Turkey. They don't just ask, "How's your family?" but are always blessing them as well: "Blessings on you, Rabia, and your sweet daughter and son, and blessings on your beloved mother. And may Allah bless you all with good fortune, good health, prosperity, and peace! *Inshallah* (God willing)!"

Then, at some point, we begin to chant together the names of the Divine — a Sufi practice called *Zikr*, remembrance of God — and talk about matters on a higher level.

"Do you have any questions, Rabia?" Halil Baba asked on this particular day; for though he once modestly said he didn't consider himself a teacher, he added gently, "perhaps a guide."

So I told him in a roundabout way that I'm often not the person I would hope to be or he sees me as, and that, in fact, I can be quite dreadful. "I always feel so sorry afterwards and swear I'll never be that way again," I said, my eyes downcast. "But then I am."

Halil Baba nodded kindly and said, "When children do something bad, they cry and say they're sorry and promise their parents they'll *never* do it again. And their parents see their good heart and intentions. So they kiss them and love them and forgive them — even knowing that they'll likely do that very thing again!"

We all laughed and Halil Baba continued, "Well, with Allah it is the same. Allah is our parent. We are all his children. And every time we sincerely say we are sorry and promise we won't do something again, Allah sees our remorse and good heart and loves us and is happy — even knowing that we'll likely do that very thing again!"

Then he told us a parable, which is how Sufis teach, through stories and fables from their oral tradition.

"There is a vast, deep ocean," he said. "And on that ocean there is a tiny island. And on that island there is a parrot sitting in a tree. And on the beak of the parrot there is a tiny speck of dirt.

"Can you see that?" Halil Baba asked, his brown eyes shining. "Well, that tiny speck of dirt is our sins. But the vast, deep ocean is Allah's compassion."

I felt my heart open — to the day, to myself, to compassion.

Then I smiled at John.

He smiled back at me.

And we both knew, most likely, I'd do that very thing again.

. . . .

"Come, come, whoever you are ....
Come, even if you have broken your vow a hundred times,
Come, come again, come."

— RUMI

MY MOTHER-IN-LAW'S BEDROOM

John's mum, Dorothy Wilcockson, always lived simply. She grew up poor in rural England and left school for work at age fourteen. By the time I met her, she was a widow in her eighties and had enough money from her pension to live nicely with her elder son, Dave, in a house by the creek in Dorking, Surrey.

Yet despite her savings, Mum lived as simply as ever. She kept their home clean and unadorned, and only bought what she truly needed. On our yearly visit, there was good food to eat, but just enough — nothing extra, no waste.

She didn't waste words, either. Each day of our visits, we'd sit together in the living room and Mum would ask us how we were feeling and how our grandchildren were, and then settle down to knit scarves — "For the old people," she'd say and then laugh, because they, in their seventies, were far younger than she. While she knitted, Dave read the horse-race results in the paper, John communicated with his computer, and I played my guitar. Now and then, someone would say something about what they were reading, or comment on the changing light outside, or Mum would say, "That's pretty, dear" about the music.

It was a routine that seemed foreign to me — raised in a Jewish home on the East Coast where you had to speak loud and fast to be heard — but I grew to love it. There was an acceptance and warmth in the silence we

shared; its peacefulness soothed me. Then, always at
4, Mum would ask, "Would you like some tea?" a few
hours before we'd begin to cook dinner. Later, we'd play
Scrabble and then go to bed.

John and I would stay in the large and airy blue room:
light-blue walls, white bedspread with blue flowers, and
sheer white curtains. I thought of Mum's room as the lilac
room because when I'd peek in, I'd get a feeling of lilac.
Perhaps it was the walls or her bedspread ... I just knew I
saw lilac.

I never entered her room until after she died. It was
such a little room, such a small space that she took for
herself, that it felt invasive to enter it when she was there.
But after she died, I wanted to see it, to know her better
in any way I could.

I walked into the room with reverence, and that
seemed right, not only because she had died, but because it
looked like a young girl's bedroom to dream in, or a nun's
room for prayer. The furnishings were sparse: a small bed
with a wooden nightstand, one chest of drawers, and a
little dressing table with a mirror. Only a few objects were
on the table: a hairbrush, some face cream, a photo of her
with her children, and two picture postcards we had sent
from Colorado. The purple curtains were homemade; the
ruffled bedspread was white with blue and lilac flowers;
and the wallpaper was a pale mauve-pink. Everything was
perfectly neat and clean and had a purpose. Nothing extra,
no waste — just a simplicity and sweetness that made her
room feel almost holy. Like Mum, it inspired me and said,
Here's another way to live.

MIRACLES TO SHARE

I was reading a book with a great title, *Stand like Mountain, Flow like Water,* by Brian Luke Seaward, and something he wrote struck me. After revealing that he'd had several mystical experiences in his life but felt guarded about sharing them since few people do, he said, "I imagine that if, indeed, we did share these on a regular basis, we might be living in a much different world. Perhaps a better world."

Now I believe, as Seaward does, that many, if not all of us, have experienced the miraculous sometime in our lives. Not just the ever-present miracles of creation, but something specific to our own life story. We might not have called it a miracle; we might have said, What an amazing coincidence, or, Thank God that happened. But maybe, just maybe, it was a miracle.

Seaward said we should speak about our miracles, perhaps so others can be open to *their* miracles or feel hope when hope is what they need. Yet sometimes it feels strange to reveal them, not just because people may roll their eyes, but because they feel like special gifts, personal and sacred, not to be talked about lightly. Still, I have two miracles I feel ready to share, maybe because they're your basic down-to-earth miracles, nothing surreal or otherworldly. They are curiously similar in the way they end. And they have a common beginning as well, for they both involve my daughter, Elise.

The first is the more mundane: I had to find a dress for Elise's wedding. My mother had subtly and not so subtly let me know that what I had worn at my son Tony's wedding was more suited for a hippie gathering — say, Woodstock. And in truth, while I loved my Navajo beads and white moccasin boots, I *had* felt a little clunky. At Elise's wedding, I would be redeemed. But then I found out that many of Elise's guests — including the partner of her father, my ex-husband — were having gowns *made*. So, the bar was raised. No problem. I was even more determined to find something special, though it wouldn't be easy, since the only style I'm comfortable in *is* kind of hippy.

John and I flew to New York a few months before the wedding to visit the kids and to find me a gown. The night before The Big Shop we were out with our friend Kenny, who asked, "What kind of dress are you looking for?" "I don't know," I said. "Something pretty." Kenny shook his head no and explained, "You need to have a clear picture of what you want if you hope to find it, especially since you've only got one day." Then he asked again, "What kind of dress are you looking for?" And I suddenly knew: "Rich gypsy!"

The next day, we were up and out before the stores opened, and our search soon led to Henri Bendel's, "New York's legendary Fifth Avenue boutique ... for trendsetting women from around the world." While John worked on his laptop, I flipped through racks of gowns, gossamer and flowing, and then spotted a shorter frock hanging on a door, perhaps rejected by someone else. It was sheer and black with red beaded roses, and a gold satin ribbon encircled its waist. It looked like a flapper's dress from the '20s, with rows of gold sequins trailing from its hem. I walked toward it, but just then a tall, friendly saleswoman appeared and asked if she could help. I told her my challenge and she guided me to a spacious, mirrored dressing room. Then she brought in a selection of gowns for me to try, including the black one with the glittery gold trim. "Can I wear black to my daughter's wedding?" I asked. "Look at the roses, look at the gold," she said. "It's hardly black." Since she looked very chic herself, like someone my mother would trust, I trusted her too.

So I tried it on and felt instant love. It reminded me of the Halloween costumes I wore in my girlhood, when I first knew I wanted to be a gypsy, not a princess. Still, as I turned this way and that in front of the mirror, making the gold sequins shimmer and swirl, I could see it wasn't quite right. That's when the saleswoman, whose name was Elaine, left the room. She returned with a handful of pins. First she pinned this and then she pinned that, until I looked in the mirror and smiled at what I saw. John agreed: "Rich gypsy. This is the one."

Elaine brought in the seamstress, who finished all the pinning, and then she handed me her card. "Fashion Consultant," it said, right next to her name; and below, it stated her email: *GypsyWoman@hotmail.com.* I was stunned, told her why, and we both laughed. But a few days later, when I called her at the store to see if the dress was ready, I was told this: "Elaine's no longer with us. She left on Sunday — the day after you bought your dress."

. . . .

The second miracle had a more somber beginning.
Elise was pregnant, an event we were all excited about.
Then, in the third month of her pregnancy, her radiolo-
gist saw something that could be worrisome and said they
needed to operate — and soon. Elise was deeply saddened,
afraid that the anesthesia could harm the fetus and also
knowing that there were other risks. I was scared too. I
didn't know anyone who had surgery while they were pregnant, and I felt so sad that she had to face this. One thing
I knew: I wanted to be there with her. But the date for the
operation was when we were leaving for Mexico, with non-
refundable tickets. And to get a ticket for New York just
a week in advance could be unbelievably costly, especially
since I didn't know when I'd want to return and needed
some leeway. On the positive side, we were booked with
Frontier Airlines, the one that calls itself "a whole different
kind of animal." Okay, Frontier, show me.

I called them and spoke with a woman named Angela,
who had a young and pleasant voice. "This is a complicated
problem, " I started off saying, but then, I felt so scared
— scared for the baby, scared for Elise — that I started to
cry. Angela made comforting sounds and encouraged me
to talk. So I explained it all: Mexico, New York, Elise, and
the baby. "Don't worry," she said gently. "I understand.
I had to have an operation in my pregnancy, too, just
around the third month. I was so scared! But now my
son is four years old and healthy as could be!" Well, this
got me crying even more. But while I was busy crying,
Angela was busy taking care of things. She made our
Mexico tickets open-dated. She booked me into New
York with their least expensive ticket. And she wrote

into the computer that for medical reasons I could change the return date at no extra cost.

"That should take care of it," she said, "and if you have any problems, just call me at this same extension. But I wrote everything down in the computer, so anyone can help you." Then she added, "Most of all, don't worry. Believe me, it will all be okay."

I hung up feeling lighter, hopeful, and blessed. And that night I wrote a thank-you note to Angela, but didn't know her last name. So I called Frontier and rang her extension. Someone named Patty answered and told me this: "Angie doesn't work here anymore. Today was her last day."

Well, Angela, wherever you are, thank you. And yes, it all turned out most beautifully okay.

. . . .

"There are only two ways to live your life.
One is as though nothing is a miracle.
The other is as though everything is a miracle."
— ALBERT EINSTEIN

GRACIAS, GRACIAS

Once a week I go to the house of Patricia Ramirez. I go because I'm part of a program called *Intercambio*: Uniting Communities, a nonprofit that started in Boulder. They train volunteers to teach English to immigrants, at whatever location meets their needs. That location is often their home, so they can learn while watching their children. I go to the home of Patricia Ramirez.

It's a small house that somehow manages to be big enough for Patricia, her husband Eddie, their three children, and niece Rosario, who came here from Mexico to find a better life. Well, Mexico just happens to be my favorite country to visit. So now, once a week, I get to feel like I'm there, in this house of bright colors that has images of Guadalupe on every wall.

Sometimes I feel tired or too busy and don't want to go. But I do. And almost always, the hour I spend there is a high point of my week. When I sit with Patricia and Rosario and they learn new words and I speak a little Spanish, I feel the contentment that comes from doing exactly what you're meant to be doing at this moment in time.

Patricia's youngest child, Marie Cruz, is always there, too, and she learns just by listening in, as she brings me her toys to show and share. The whole family likes to share. It's impossible to leave without them offering food and drink or a homemade gift.

One week I went there on a Saturday, and that was the best time of all. When I entered their house, I was embraced with chatter, laughter, and good smells. Rosario and Patricia were in the kitchen, cooking a special soup made with lemons, pork, cilantro, and whole ears of corn. Eddie was sitting at the dining-room table helping his son, Eddie Jr., with his schoolwork, while teenager Kathy sat on the sofa, chatting endlessly on her cell phone. The TV was playing a *telenovela,* Mexican soap opera, and Marie Cruz was playing with a friend and her many toys. I went upstairs with my two students, where we sat on a bed as they read from *Frog and Toad Are Friends*, a children's book I love. We also talked about our lives so they could practice speaking English. They spoke of growing up in a dusty rural village, where daily outings to street markets gave them mangos, chilies, and a sense of community.

When I left that day, Patricia gave me a large container filled with the freshly made soup and, as always, said "*gracias!*" many times. "*Gracias*, Rivvy. *Gracias* for coming. *Gracias.*" I breathed in the smells of the soup, the children's laughter, the faith, the noise, and the family's love, and I said "*gracias*" too.

LIFE, DEATH, AND LAUGHTER

Some of the best times of my life have been times of all-out laughter. Laughing until I cry when I'm with my sister Susan, who no matter what can get me laughing — at life, or love, or at myself. And laughing growing up because my father, Bernie Feldman, was the funniest man I ever knew. He was our live-in Jewish comedian, and he could tell jokes like no one else.

In Jewish tradition, the best jokes are stories, passed on with the right accents, pacing, and suspense. A Catholic friend of mine, being thoughtful, once sent me an email of fifty Jewish jokes. None of them seemed funny. You've got to be there; they've got to be told; and no one told them like my dad.

My father died young, after many years of terrible pain. When his emphysema worsened and he was in Abington Hospital's intensive care unit, John and I flew there to visit him and quietly entered his room — where he was just beginning to feel better, but pretended for our sake to be feeling worse ("*Oy!*" he moaned. "*Oy vey!*"). He then proceeded to tell us a story ("This is true," he'd always say first), which evolved into a raunchy joke about reincarnated rabbits. It was one of his best, and he told it pitch perfect, until the nurse came by to scold us because we were laughing so loudly.

"Some people here are critically ill!" she said, forgetting that one of them was Dad.

It wasn't long after he died that his doctors told Mom how much they missed him. They missed his spirit and courage ... and how he always made them laugh.

I guess you could live a sacred life without laughter. But tell me this: Why would you want to?

. . . .

"The Creator made humans able to walk and talk, to see and hear ... to do everything. But the Creator wasn't satisfied. Finally, the Creator made humans laugh, and when they laughed and laughed, the Creator said, 'Now you are fit to live.'"

— TRADITIONAL APACHE STORY

. . .

I was going to tell you the joke about the rabbits.
But, like I said, you've got to be there.

A GOOD DAY

I was feeling overwhelmed — finishing a community project; preparing for our grandchildren's first visit to Boulder; cleaning the house and cooking dinner; watering the sunroom plants (how did we get so many?); booking airline tickets to London to attend our niece's wedding…. I was also feeling it was a lost day because I wasn't doing my work.

Then I remembered Susan Jeffers' advice in her book *End the Struggle and Dance with Life*. Create a *huge* life, she says, not one focused solely on goals and aspirations, but one that is "filled with many *equally important* components." "It's *all* important," she reminds us, meaning the friends, the home, the family … the work, the world, and the fun.

I had remembered that it's important to keep a sense of balance and not just work, but I'd forgotten that each part of the circle gets equal credit.

So I reviewed my day — what I had done and what I was doing — and saw that it was all good. Then I put on a Beatles CD and started dancing as I cooked, feeling grateful for these many parts of my life. I loved how the house looked so neat and clean. I was relieved that we were finally set for Gillian's wedding. The rice and beans smelled spicy and nourishing. And as I watered the plants, I enjoyed their beauty and touched their soft leaves.

This is it, I thought. This is my life. And sometimes, living sacred just means being present — moment to moment, day by day.

. . . .

When my grandson Brendan was four-and-a-half, I asked him if he ever had a bad day. "No," he said. "Never?" I questioned. He thought a bit and then said, "Yeah, but it ended good."

THE LORD IS WITH ME...
OR WHATEVER

When my mother was eighty, she read a line in a hymn that she particularly liked. In English it meant: "The Lord is with me, I shall not fear." And since my mother doesn't read Hebrew, she looked at its transliteration and found that to be: "*Adonai lee-la ear-ah.*" Soon, she started saying it to all of us whenever we were about to fly, or have surgery, or felt scared in any way. "Let's say it together," she'd insist, and we'd recite along with her, "*Adonai lee-la ear-ah*" — The Lord is with me. I shall not fear." It kind of became our family prayer.

I liked it, and I liked saying it with her — so much so that I'd call her from my cell phone each time I'd board a plane. We'd say those words together and I'd feel a wondrous calm.

Then, one day, I found that line in a prayer book. But the true transliteration was "*Adonai lee-*V'LOW *ear-ah*" and not "*Adonai lee-*LA *ear-ah.*" So! All these years we'd been saying the wrong words, and God knows what they meant. Some family prayer!

I didn't want to tell Mom and get her upset. Still, I was a little annoyed by her habit of muddling up words (a habit I've inherited that annoys my daughter). So I decided that whenever we'd say it together, I'd say it correctly and *loudly,* thinking sooner or later she'd switch to the right words. But she didn't. I worried it wouldn't work for her — I mean, if a mantra has powers, then it helps to say the right words, no?

Then I read a Zen story about a poor peasant who wandered for miles to find a Master and ask for his guidance. The Master asked him if he had a spiritual practice. The peasant said he had one prayer that he'd repeat all day, which he then recited for the Master. "No!" the Master shouted, "You've got it wrong! That prayer goes like this." He taught the peasant the correct prayer and felt relieved that he helped save this poor man's soul. The peasant thanked him gratefully and walked away. But when he reached the river, he just kept on walking, walking on water as if it were land. When the Master saw this, he ran after the peasant shouting, "Wait! Forget what I said! Stick to your old prayer, and never stop!"

So my mom still says "*Adonai lee*-LA *ear-ah*," and now I do too. It's catchy, you know? And so is her faith.

DO THE RIGHT THING

I was a beatnik in college. I wore black tights, smoked French cigarettes, and majored in philosophy. The boys I dated also majored in "phil." It felt very Jean Paul Sartre/Simone de Beauvoir. But, as my mother noted, it didn't put me on a career track. It didn't even have staying power. I read ump-teen books, yet all I remember now are a few sound bites ("God is dead" — Nietzsche), or some motif, like the caves in Plato's *Republic*. Worse still, I recall endless discussions on What Is Real and little guidance on What Is Right or how to do the right thing. With one exception, Kant's categorical imperative. It goes like this:

> *"Act only according to that maxim whereby you can at the same time will that it should become a universal law."*

Right. In poor-man's English that means: Before doing anything, you need to imagine everyone else doing the same thing and it still being okay. Kant called this the ultimate moral dictum, and I called it brilliant. I could no longer tell "just one person" a piece of gossip or not speak out if our government did something grievously wrong. It was Kant's categorical imperative that helped me explain to my second-grade students why littering "just one candy wrapper" could lead to an environmental disaster. And it was Kant's C.I. that let me tell my own young children that they couldn't pick "just one flower" from Central Park, because if everyone did it, there'd be no flowers left.

"But ..." Tony protested, "not everyone *is* going to do it."

"Tony," I answered, "don't be a smartass."

Still, there are conflicts that require a more subtle measure than Kant proposed. For those, I go to my heart or gut. Deepak Chopra says that sensations in our body can help us make the right choice. I find it's true. As I prepare to heal a friendship or share something I've re-pressed, I imagine what I'm about to say or do and check how it feels inside. If it feels bad, I drop it; if it feels good, I move ahead.

And then, in those times when I'm truly confused — or know what to do, but feel too angry to do it — I reflect on a picture on my office wall. A sepia print from the 1920s, it shows a Native American man looking up at the mountains and the words below it say, "When in doubt, go higher." So I do. I go higher and reach for my spirit. And the view from there is all I need to do the right thing.

. . . .

Reach higher, Reach for your soul.

— RUMI
*(Billboard sign on boardwalk
at Venice Beach, Los Angeles)*

THIS, TOO, SHALL PASS

I felt a little bad when *AARP, The Magazine* started coming in the mail. It arrived spontaneously one day as if to announce: You're old! Think retired! Think golf! Think death! And it kept on coming, bimonthly, in case I might forget. Then, in Spring 2006, it featured an interview with His Holiness, the Dalai Lama of Tibet. This was good news. I didn't mind being part of the AARP gang if the Dalai Lama was on board. Seeing his blissful, smiling face on the cover seemed so incongruous that it was perfect. So was the interview.

> *"**AARP**: When you have negative emotions, what are they?*
> ***The Dalai Lama**: Anger. Jealousy. And some feelings of hopelessness."*

Hmm, I thought. If even His Holiness has moments of anger, jealousy, and hopelessness, then I don't have to feel so bad when I do too.

And then it got even better. He used his Buddhist logic to explain why you can't feel hopeless for long:

> *"If some bad things come and remain forever, there is a certain reason to feel hopelessness. But this doesn't happen. Things are always moving, always changing. If we envision that, there is no reason to feel hopeless."*

So. There you have it. And if I ever need proof of the changing flow of life, all I need do is read my old journals:

> *February 1: I'm so depressed, everything looks bad, I'm angry at J., can't see my way out....*

> *February 2: Oh thank you, Great Spirit, for this wonderful day. I feel blessed, I love J., Life is good....*

Truth is, all things are passing, even hopelessness, and when you remember that, it helps it pass sooner.

But if you're like me, there's still a problem. When lost in darkness, I tend to forget that dawn is coming, or there's light in the tunnel, or any other helpful saying. There's something about hopelessness that just feels ... well, *hopeless*.

Then I read a story about King Solomon that kind of went like this:

> *One day the King was feeling very down. He gathered his ministers and said, "Whenever I feel happy, I'm afraid it won't last. But when I feel sadness, I fear it won't end. Find me the answer to this suffering."*

> *His ministers scattered throughout the country, searching for the wisdom or magic that would ease the King's pain. Finally, one of them met an old jeweler who carved on a simple gold ring the Hebrew inscription "gam zeh ya'avor" — "This, too, shall pass."*

> *When the King received the ring and read the inscription, he knew it was magical. For his sadness turned to*

> *joy, his joy turned to sadness, and then both gave way to*
> *peace and surrender.*

Good enough for King Solomon, good enough for me. I bought a ring with one stone to remember, "This, too, shall pass."

And sooner or later, it always does.

POCO A POCO

After writing thirty-some stories for this book, I got stuck. Sure, I had more recipes to share, but no stories to make them come alive. Great, I thought, just what people need, another "Do This" list of spiritual advice that would sound a million times better coming from the Dalai Lama than Rivvy Neshama ("Rivvy *who*?"). Fortunately, I had lots of ways to procrastinate and avoid facing just how stuck I was.

But the day of reckoning came: I had put aside four hours to write, and maybe I would have (really) if my computer hadn't suddenly gone black while making sounds like a vacuum cleaner. I was also in a jealous, edgy, angry mood, not the best place from which to write a book on sacred living.

Then my friend Ellie called and we shared updates on our lives. I sadly mentioned the book and being stuck, cut off from the flow.

"Don't lose faith," Ellie said. "Inspiration comes and goes. Just take it *poco a poco*. Your life will show you what to write."

"*Poco a poco*," I said. "Little by little ... step by step. That's one of them!" A recipe I wanted to share. That if you resolve to do something but have trouble doing it, or feel overwhelmed and don't know where to begin, or you're lost in darkness and can't find the light … not to worry. Just keep the faith and move forward, one step at a time.

There was a game we played as kids in the alley behind my house. It was called "Mother, May I?" and you asked the leader, who stood on a chalk line far out in front, "Mother, may I take two giant steps?" Then, if they said "no," you might ask to take "ten baby steps" or "three scissor steps," and the first one to reach the leader won.

I don't remember the rules exactly, but I do remember this: It didn't matter so much what *kind* of steps you took, just so long as you kept moving forward, little by little, till you finally reached the line. And the nice thing was that everyone got there, sooner or later. The game didn't end until they did.

WORDS TO LIVE BY

I'm not sure who gave me this recipe or when I started
using it, but I find it helpful to post words of guidance or
inspiration around the house — on mirrors, walls, or by
my computer. Some of them I cut out from magazines;
others are from cards or posters; and a few are quota-
tions I copied from books. I don't always notice them,
but when I do, they wake me up and give my spirit a lift.

A NEW YEAR'S GREETING

Every new year — Chinese New Year, that is — we get a
hand-printed greeting card from our acupuncturist, David
Scrimgeour. Each has a picture of the animal that year rep-
resents in Chinese tradition (say, The Year of the Horse),
along with some words of wisdom passed on by David.

I'm always surprised by the animals the Chinese
chose to honor. Given their twelve-year cycle for naming
the years, they could have picked all elegant or powerful
ones: Lion, Horse, Swan. But instead they've included
the Rat, the Monkey, the Rooster. There's something
very inclusive about that. It reminds me that all beings,
no matter how lowly they seem, have their own unique
virtues and redeeming qualities. Go, Rat!

Anyway, one card David sent us said:

"Trust in the Universe and Move Forward in Your life."

I think it came in the Year of the Pig, but I taped it on my desk since its wisdom holds forever.

ONE DAY AT A TIME

I always liked the "Serenity Prayer," often attributed to Reinhold Niebuhr:

> *"God grant me the serenity to accept the things I cannot change,*
> *Courage to change what I can,*
> *And the wisdom to know the difference."*

My daughter, Elise, sent it to me once on a greeting card, and I hung it on my office wall. It felt ennobling, though a bit daunting. I mean, it's not easy to accept what we cannot change, right?

Later, I found out that the prayer is an integral part of Alcoholics Anonymous and other 12-step programs, and some meetings end with all members reciting it.

Later still, I was at an art show where my friend Kristine Smock had created wrought iron sculptures of this prayer: the words themselves surrounded by animals of the land, sea, and air. That's when I found out that the Serenity Prayer has a tagline: *"Living one day at a time."* Kristine had made a sculpture of this phrase, too, and that's the one we bought to hang in our home. Almost anything seems possible to change or accept when I take life "one day at a time."

DESIDERATA

Back in the sixties, nearly every psychedelic shop had a copy of "Desiderata" for sale, amongst the neon posters and hashish pipes. It was a prose poem of prayerful advice, often printed on imitation parchment paper, and at the bottom it said, "Found in Old St. Paul's Church. Dated 1692." I bought a copy, framed it, and hung it in my home. Its guidance felt so relevant and so in tune with my flower-child sentiments that every time I read it I'd say "Wow!" It seemed way cool and mystical that someone wrote this in the 17th century. It also seemed suspect. I could easily picture some fellow hippie writing this and then deciding it would sell better if people thought it was ancient wisdom found in some church. Which is probably true, but doesn't seem fair. If words are wise, why should it matter who said them or when? But I guess it does, since I liked to believe it was written eons ago and found in Old St. Paul's.

Then, around the millennium, I received about ten copies of an email that was said to be "what the Dalai Lama has to say on the millennium" and gave a list of nineteen instructions for life. Now I had heard the Dalai Lama is a fan of e-mail, but I somehow didn't see him writing this list — especially when the last item was "Approach love and cooking with reckless abandon!" Which made me question again the source of the "Desiderata." So I did some research and here's what I found:

The "Desiderata," which is Latin for "things to be desired," was written by Max Ehrmann in the 1920s. Max was a poet and attorney from Terre Haute, Indiana. Apparently, a rector of St. Paul's Church in Baltimore, Maryland, found the poem in 1959, printed it up for his congregants, and noted on the top "Old St. Paul's Church, Baltimore A.C. 1692," since his church was founded in 1692. This led to the later confusion.

Okay, "Written by a Hoosier Lawyer. Dated 1927" doesn't quite have the charm of "Found in Old St. Paul's Church. Dated 1692." Nonetheless, I continue to love and be inspired by the "Desiderata." It still hangs in our home, and whenever I read it, one line will stand out as the perfect message I need at that time.

For those of you who missed the sixties, here it is:

DESIDERATA

Go placidly amid the noise and the haste, and remember what peace there may be in silence.

As far as possible, without surrender, be on good terms with all persons. Speak your truth quietly and clearly; and listen to others, even to the dull and the ignorant; they too have their story. Avoid loud and aggressive persons; they are vexations to the spirit.

If you compare yourself with others, you may become vain or bitter, for always there will be greater and lesser persons than yourself. Enjoy your achievements as well as your plans. Keep interested in your own career, however humble; it is a real possession in the changing fortunes of time.

Exercise caution in your business affairs, for the world is full of trickery. But let this not blind you to what virtue there is; many persons strive for high ideals, and everywhere life is full of heroism. Be yourself. Especially do not feign affection. Neither be cynical about love, for in the face of all aridity and disenchantment, it is as perennial as the grass.

Take kindly the counsel of the years, gracefully surrendering the things of youth. Nurture strength of spirit to shield you in sudden misfortune. But do not distress yourself with dark imaginings. Many fears are born of fatigue and loneliness.

Beyond a wholesome discipline, be gentle with yourself. You are a child of the universe, no less than the trees and the stars; you have a right to be here. And whether or not it is clear to you, no doubt the universe is unfolding as it should.

Therefore be at peace with God, whatever you conceive Him to be. And whatever your labors and aspirations, in the noisy confusion of life, keep peace in your soul.

With all its sham, drudgery, and broken dreams, it is still a beautiful world.

Be cheerful. Strive to be happy.

Part Two

THE SUN
IS RISING

Open to the dawning
of a brand new day.

HELLO TO THE SUN

I once spent a week at an ashram in the Bahamas. The worst part was being woken at 5 a.m. to chant outside on the chilly beach. The best part was being woken at 5 a.m. to get to watch the rising sun.

So there I was, sitting cross-legged with some fifty other seekers, chanting *Hare Krishna,* and shivering in the cold. I watched the dark sky grow lighter and greyer, and then, more pleasingly, pinker and brighter. But where was the sun? Seagulls were calling, the sky was changing colors, and I'm thinking, What's going on? By the time the sun appears, it will be, like, no big deal.

I pulled my sweater tighter, while casting furtive, longing glances at Club Med a few doors down, and that's when I saw it. On the horizon of turquoise waters, a gold arc suddenly appeared, and slowly, slowly, the sun rose — and I got it. A sunrise is the exact opposite of a sunset; instead of the sun going down in the west followed by streaks of color, you get a glorious lightshow in the east announcing its arrival: Here comes the Sun!

I remembered that years later when I picked up a children's book called *The Way to Start a Day.* Page one showed a beautiful sunrise and said:

> *"The way to start a day*
> *is this —*

Go outside
and face the east
and greet the sun
with some kind of
blessing
or chant
or song
that you made yourself
and keep for
early morning."

There were drawings of Africans drumming, of women offering flowers at shrines in India, of Aztecs playing songs on their flutes ... of people from all over the world sharing this ancient ritual: to honor that moment when the sun first appears.

Okay, I was sold. I wouldn't necessarily get up at dawn (I'm a night person, always was), but I would bless the sun each morning in person.

At first, I simply stood outside on our patio and said, "Hi, Sun! Thanks for coming." But soon this evolved into a more native routine.

I begin by holding my palms together as I face the rising sun. "Hello to the sun!" I say, while lifting my arms high in a sweeping circle. Then I turn to greet all four directions, with words that reflect their different aspects and gifts: "Hello to the East! Innocence, new beginnings. Blessings on the East." "Hello to the South! Heart opening, loving-kindness...." I also salute the other three directions: "Hello above" (the sky), "Hello below" (the earth), and "Hello within" (the center, the heart).

Looking around, I then say "Hello to the flowers and trees" as I take in their beauty, and "Hello to the birds and all the animals" as I listen for their sounds.

My salutation ends with two bows and a prayer:

"Thank you for this world.

Thank you for this day.

It's a good day to die!

It's a good day to live!"

I do this every morning, no matter how late I get moving. It helps me feel fresh, uplifted, and open. Open to the dawning of a brand-new day.

THE FIRST FEW STEPS

It's a new day. You wake up feeling great and excited ...
or maybe tired and overwhelmed. No matter. Here are
some ways to raise your spirits. What works best, I find,
is to pick one or a few, make them yours, and do them
often — until they become your morning ritual. Still,
here's an honest disclaimer: Some days, for me, nothing
works. I wake up growling, and it's just a bad day. That
said, read on:

GIVE THANKS
You might sit by a candle or simply sit up in bed and say
thanks in whatever way feels right.

> *Gracias, Papito Dios, por el milagro de un otro dia de la vida.*
> Thank you, dearest God, for the miracle of an-
> other day of life.

MAKE A VOW ABOUT HOW YOU WANT TO LIVE THIS DAY
Thich Nhat Hanh, a Buddhist monk and peace activist from
Vietnam, offers *gathas,* short verses, to guide us through the
day. Here's one he suggests we might start with:

> *"Waking up this morning, I smile.*
> *Twenty-four brand new hours are before me.*
> *I vow to live fully each moment*
> *and to look at all beings with eyes of compassion."*

I've shortened this to say: "*I vow to live fully and view all beings with compassion, including myself.*"

OR LET AN AFFIRMATION COME TO YOU

It can be a different one or several each day. Affirm out loud whatever you want to be feeling or creating.

> *My life is filled with gratitude and love.*
> *I am healthy, strong, and radiantly alive.*
> *I'm living with kindness and calmness and faith.*

MEDITATE

Many teachers suggest that you start and end the day with meditation: a way to frame your day with peace.

PRAY

Morning is also a good time for prayer, and prayer can take any form you wish: giving thanks, sending love and healing thoughts to others, affirming or requesting that which you need, or simply talking with your higher self or whatever divine presence you believe in or perceive.

REMEMBER YOUR DREAMS

Write them down in a dream book you keep by your bed, or say them out loud and listen for their message. If the dream felt bad or disturbing, think of a way to continue it that turns out well. Or look for a symbol or person in the dream that you feel good about and focus on that.

DO YOGA OR TAI CHI

Hatha yoga and tai chi are ways to wake up your body and soul. Just ten minutes of poses or a few sets of Sun Salutations are all it takes to feel calmer and focused.

OR GET GROUNDED IN YOUR BODY SOME OTHER WAY

You might sit still, watch your breath as it goes in and out, and feel the calm. Or take a walk or jog outside amid the sounds and smells of the morning waking up.

READ

Our friends Jane and Bo start each morning together, reading something inspirational — "something from 12-step and then something Buddhist." I keep inspirational books by my bedside, open one up to any page, and read the message. It's always right; it always works.

LISTEN TO MUSIC

Put on music you love to set the tone of your day.

VISUALIZE

While lying in bed, close your eyes, take some deep breaths, and picture yourself somewhere beautiful, say, a beach in Hawaii. Then imagine the sun streaming golden light through you, all through your body and out through your fingers and toes, cleansing you and clearing away any tension.

GREET WITH GLADNESS

This is very British, "be-of-good-cheer" advice, suggested by my English friend Helen. If you have a partner or child, she says, wake them or greet them with a glad heart (especially if you live in England, where the skies are often grey). And sure enough, John, my English husband, always smiles at me each morning, looks out at our Colorado sky, and if just a speck of blue is present, he says, "It's a beautiful day." That's right, even if I'm growling, that's what he says.

Part Three

ANIMAL CHATS
AND OTHER
UNIONS WITH
NATURE

One autumn, while hiking in Shropshire,
we wandered into a flock of sheep.
A few were scared and walked off,
sheep-like. But they kept turning to
look back, as curious as we were.

IN THE WOODS

In 1698, in a small town in the Ukraine, Israel ben Eliezer was born. The legends say he was different from other children: While they were busy playing, he would wander into the woods and stay there for hours talking to God.

Israel grew up to be a beloved rabbi. People called him the Ba'al Shem Tov, Master of the Good Name, and he was the founder of Hasidism, a mystical movement in Judaism. He taught his followers to be on the lookout for God, who is everywhere, he said, in everyone and everything.

Until the end of his life, the Ba'al Shem continued his forays into the woods to meditate and talk freely with God. One day a friend asked him, "Izzy, if God is everywhere, why go in the woods to pray?" The Ba'al Shem answered, "It's true, my friend, God is everywhere. But it's easiest, for me, to find him in the woods."

When I was a kid in Philly, my favorite adventures were with my cousin Eddie: bike trips to Carpenter's Woods. We'd leave the busy streets and honking cars of Germantown and soon hear only silence or the rushing water of the creek. Resting our bikes on the fern-covered ground, we'd hike through this forest with its shafts of light. For a city girl, those times were a source of peace, and a sense of something much bigger than myself.

Years later, I discovered that those feelings could be deepened by going camping. So when I moved to

Boulder, where the plains meet the mountains, John
and I vowed to camp out every autumn. It's a vow I often
remind him of: "Time for our annual camping trip!" —
annual in that we plan one every year, but rarely actually
go. Why? Because like many things in life, camping is
a lot more fun in the planning stage. And half the fun
is in replying, "What are we doing this weekend? Oh,
we're going campin'." Said with subtle overtones at once
macho and righteous.

Our back-in-Manhattan friends — who have avoided
such outings ever since they were kids sent to summer
camp in the Catskills — are impressed. Our here-
in-Boulder friends — who prefer two-week treks to
two-night car camping — are not. Still, they are kindly
solicitous: "Be sure to keep all your food in the car so
you won't attract bears." Right, I nod.

Bears?! Why do I always forget little details like
bears? Which brings me to the fantasizing. I mean, I
always picture us tenting on the perfect site: on top of
a hill amid a grove of fir trees. There we are, John and
I, sitting around the starry-night campfire, hearing the
primal sounds of elks bugling (if we're lucky), and then
falling into a deep sleep in our cozy tent.

Now, here's what happened the last time we camped:
It took three hours to pack our car with every possible
necessity and a surplus of canned food, and by the time
we arrived at Rocky Mountain National Park, we were
assigned the only site left: a patch of dirt in the woods
right under the power line. "No problem," said my ever-
optimistic husband. "The only time we'll be in the tent is
when we're sleeping. Let's go on a beautiful hike."

Good idea, until it started raining. Sloshing through mud, we returned to our campsite and soon surrendered any dreams of a campfire. Stashing our marshmallows into the car, we drove four miles to find a good diner.

Later, back in the tent, I suddenly remembered why we rarely go camping: achy back from lying on hard dirt floor; going to the bathroom in the cold, rainy night; woken every ten minutes by those damn bugling elks. I was not a happy camper.

Truth is, when I lived in Manhattan where museums are abundant, I rarely went to museums. But surrounded by all that art, I felt very "artsy." And now, surrounded by all these mountains, I feel very "campy." So why, I ask myself, do we actually have to go?

Maybe it's because I've reached an age where I know I'm mortal, and I don't want my last words to be: "I wish we had camped out more."

Or maybe it's because even last time, there were moments — the totally dark and silent night; being woken at dawn by two calling crows; a cool, misty morning that smelled of pines — moments of sensing that God is everywhere. And, like the Ba'al Shem Tov, I tend to find him in the woods.

ANIMAL CHATS

One reason I fell in love with John was he talked to animals. Nothing heavy, just "Hello, Mr. Squirrel. How are you today?" or "Hi, Miss Robin, Welcome back!" I found it endearing and, like him, very English — in a Peter Rabbit kind of way. In fact, when we visited the village where John was born, it was like stepping into a Beatrix Potter book. There were rabbits and ducks wherever I looked. And on the hillside nearby, I spotted some sheep.

That was no big deal since sheep are found all over England, where they're said to outnumber people. One autumn, while hiking in Shropshire, we wandered into a flock of them. They stared at us, and we stared back. Then I started to sing softly so they wouldn't be afraid. A few were still scared and walked off, one after the other, sheep-like. But they kept turning to look back, as curious as we were.

Sheep aren't the only animals I've reached out to. After reading a book that said we can communicate with all species, I tried it first with bugs. I'd ask certain flies to alight on my hand and stand still — and they would! I could see their antennas going, boom, boom, and for the first time I felt there was spirit in those flies, who were looking at me as surely as I was looking at them.

I do believe it's possible to converse with all animals, perhaps more telepathically than verbally. The first time John and I went hiking in Hall Ranch, in the mountains near Lyons, Colorado, we were expecting to see an abundance of wildlife since it offered new trails and had long been left wild. Yet in two hours of hiking, we saw nothing but trees, even when we stood still and were quiet. So I called out to the wild ones, silently, asking them to join us. Within minutes, we spotted a lizard, a snake, a rabbit ... and then a herd of deer ran leaping along the red cliffs above us. My heart leapt too.

I've also noticed that when John goes off traveling or I'm facing some crisis, the neighborhood deer come to sleep on our lawn. I'm not aware that I've called them, yet they come, like a faithful dog that knows when it's needed.

There are some species though — say, earwigs — that I have little interest in talking to. Especially when they enter our home. Still, I try to honor all living things, so instead of killing them, I ask them to leave, and if they don't, I carry them out (well, have John carry them out). If I do choose to kill, I offer an apology or prayer, the way the Indians did when they killed buffalo for meat. The Native People honor the buffalo and call him their brother. They believe we are all related, four-footed as well as two-footed creatures, along with plants and trees, sky and earth ... and even my mean third-grade teacher, Miss Brown. All of us, linked together, in an inextricable Hoop of Life.

Nowadays, I speak to animals as much as John does. "Hi, Magpie," I say. "Hello, Bees." And when the deer come to graze on our lawn, I talk to them in a quiet tone, as I've been taught you should. "No worries," I assure them. "Glad you're here. You can eat the grass, but stay out of the flowers." Their ears perk up attentively, and then they eat the flowers.

ODES TO A GARDEN

SOIL TIME

I met Majid at a Sufi ceremony — a *Zjkr,* which means remembrance, remembrance of God. We chanted and danced and whirled like dervishes, with each turn lifting us higher. Then we sat on exotic rugs and ate exotic treats: almonds and figs, and pastries with honey. All in remembrance of God. Yum.

It was at a spring *Zjkr* that I met Majid, a noble-looking man in his thirties. He had moved to Boulder from Iran and was studying to be a landscape architect. He was looking for work, and my garden was looking for help.

One week later, Majid came and transplanted some forget-me-nots from our backyard to the front so we could see those blue beauties more clearly. I helped pat down the dirt and said a blessing, "Take root and live. We love you. Be happy."

Majid told me that Islam says whoever works in the soil is closest to Allah. He enjoys researching plants and making landscape drawings. But to feel good, he said, he needs his hands in the soil.

I feel the same. Like a kid making mud pies, I'm in bliss when my hands are in dirt — touching it, smelling its earthy smell, and watching the hidden world of worms and insects beneath. And if I'm feeling tense, there's nothing like digging up weeds to feel clear again and present.

Soil time. Close to the earth. Closest to Allah.

PLANTING

I read a story once about a woman who moved often yet planted gardens wherever she lived. She didn't mind that she was moving on and leaving them behind. She didn't mind doing all that work for results she might never see. Her happiness came, she said, from making the world more beautiful.

WATERING

Every June morning, I rise early and go to the garden to water the budding flowers and newborn vegetables before the sun gets too hot. Everything is serene at this hour, as the sky slowly opens and the earth wakes up. I hold the hose and water deeply, standing still, almost in a trance. Between the rows of chard I see a neon-blue dragonfly sipping nectar from a rose. The birds are chirping, the butterflies playing, and soon I am lost in the buzz of the bees. All the world is singing, it seems, singing thank you for this day.

By late August, though, the joy of watering wears thin. "Did you water the plants?" I ask John hopefully, since it's already 9 a.m. and the sun is getting hot. "No, I was too busy," he says. So I stump out to the garden where most things now look a little old and withered and I'm thinking, Oh, they're gonna die soon anyway, why bother.

Then a tiny green hummingbird lands on our floppy comfrey plant, dips into its purple flowers, hovers above it, and leaves.

Okay guys, I'm back, hose in hand, ready to water.

POPPIES

Everyone in Boulder had poppies — masses of poppies — everyone except us. "Take ours!" neighbors implored. "They're like weeds!" So I picked a few and tried to transplant them in different parts of our meadow. No luck. Then I sowed their seeds and waited for spring. Still no luck. Finally, after three years of poppy mistrials, we planted the seeds in the right place at the right time and up they popped.

And once up, they were unstoppable, producing more and more each year. I love to see them from my office window, a splash of orange against green grass and blue sky. But it's up close that they're outrageous, with their huge, ruffled petals, shiny black design, and a flurry of seeds circling one purple star.

The Buddha said, "If we could see the miracle of a single flower clearly, our whole life would change." I think he was looking at poppies.

SIMPLE PLEASURES

It wasn't until I moved to Boulder that I discovered the joys of a clothesline. When John first asked me to leave Manhattan and join him out West, I pictured him fetching me in a covered wagon. Leaving the city that never sleeps for what was then a sleepy town made me feel like a pioneer woman ("Rivvy of the Prairies"), and so did using a clothesline. I guess I was finally learning the simple tasks of daily life. And after years of urban living, I relished each old-fashioned chore.

I loved standing barefoot in the grass, using wooden pegs to hang our sheets. I delighted in watching them blow in the wind as the sun and air naturally dried them. And later, when I made our bed, I savored their fresh, sweet scent and remembered how, as a child, I would walk between and smell the sheets my mother hung to dry.

Now, I admit it: The clothesline broke and I reunited with our electric dryer. No worries, I told John. We can still save energy. I'll just wash less often … and vacuum less too!

But every now and then, I still hang something out to dry, and that always feels right. And when we'd phone John's ninety-seven-year-old mother in England, she'd often tell us she was just outside, hanging the wash to dry. She never did anything but. So this one's a recipe from Dorothy Wilcockson ("Dorothy of Mole Valley"), who knew the joy of simple pleasures.

THE BIRD CONNECTION

Few things cheer me as instantly as birds. When a flock of them rise all at once from a tree, chattering away as they soar ever higher, I can't stop myself from smiling.

Sometimes I sit on a bench in our yard, listening to the songs of our neighborhood birds and noting what they're up to. I've seen small birds hitch a ride on larger ones. I've seen robins courting, the female flirting but flying away once the male approaches, in some ritual that's not unlike our own. And I once saw a gang of magpies chase a squirrel who dared to bother them while they were eating.

To witness all this interaction feels humbling: Our Earth is so rich; there's so much I don't know. Bird watching is a way to learn more.

The fun begins by sitting still and being allowed into their world. There's also the pleasure of using a field guide to discover the names of birds you don't know. Flipping through the pages is like doing a puzzle ... and then, aha! This picture and description fit the bill (so to speak). That handsome black bird with red on its wings is called a "Red-winged blackbird." Well named! I say it a few times and write it down, grateful that some people actually recorded the names and traits of thousands of species.

Once you get to know your birds better, you start to notice their different ways; they're not just all "birds." And, just as with people, you will have your favorites.

I'm partial to robins because they seem more trusting. Most of the birds that hang out in our garden fly away fast when I appear. But when a robin is around doing its business (usually digging for worms) and I come out to do my business (usually digging for weeds), the robin cocks its head as if to say hi and doesn't fly away. We're there together, *muy simpatico,* each doing our own thing.

On the other hand, one bird I wasn't crazy about is the grackle. It makes a crackling (grackling?) kind of noise, and it appears to be mean. Grackles first came to our bird feeder one May morning and immediately started bombing down on smaller birds — sweet finches, innocent sparrows — to scare them away. In a few days, the turf was theirs. I was not pleased. All my joy of watching an array of birds at the feeder was being ruined by a few neighborhood thugs!

I called our local Wild Bird Center to complain and see what I could do. The man who answered informed me that grackles are not native to Boulder but started coming here after some folks planted *trees* that are not native — trees from back East that the grackles prefer, namely, Austrian pines. Yes, I confessed, we planted two of them right by the house and they're now 12 feet tall, elegant, and strong.

So, I asked, how can I get rid of the grackles? "Cut down the pines," he said. Right. Thanks.

"Why do you want to get rid of them?" he asked, sensing I was not about to grab an axe. "They have a right to be here, as much as all the other birds." They're pushing *out* all the other birds, I argued. They're mean and aggressive and greedy. "Hmm," said their defender.

"They probably built a nest nearby and they're protecting it. That's why they're chasing off the other birds. It's their parental instinct."

Well, that made them more sympathetic in my eyes, if it were in fact true. And a few weeks later, I found out it was! I heard tiny grackles grackling and saw something I'd never seen before: Grackle after grackle would come feed the little ones; not just the mother or father as I'd observed with other birds, but the whole grackle clan, bringing worms to drop into the mouths of the babes.

So this is a shout-out for grackles. Add a chair to the table and welcome them too.

. . . .

Thank you for the birds that sing,
Thank you, God, for everything!

WITH BEAUTY MAY I WALK

Around the time we were thinking of moving back East, back to family, our friend Carrie took John and me to a summer art show. It was called "Dual Visions," and it featured the work of artist couples. Each couple had written a statement as well, describing what inspired them to create and how their partner's vision influenced their own. One couple wrote that nothing inspired them more than the beauty of nature: "It reminds us to make our life beautiful, whether it be the garden, our home, the art we make, or a dinner with close friends."

Carrie and her husband, Hal, were the oldest couple whose work was displayed. Carrie was eighty, but still had bangs and the air of a tomboy. With her lilting laugh and endless curiosity, she seemed to be forever young. Hal, her longtime partner in art and adventures, had died at eighty-four, one year before the show.

An environmentalist and geologist, Hal had also been a photographer. He loved the native beauty of our world and wanted to preserve it. To realize that goal, he photographed some of the most untouched places on Earth for The Nature Conservancy, an organization that raises money to purchase such land and protect it. The "Dual Vision" show displayed a few of Hal's photographs of woodlands and wilderness. Shot in black and white, each rock and tree looked ancient, and there was drama played out between shadow and light. Hal had written before he died that his aim was twofold: to capture the beauty and to enhance it by the way he framed each photo.

Carrie's pictures were also of trees and rocks and wildland, but hers were charcoal sketches, softer and more intimate, and her aim was to lose herself — or find herself — in nature. "Hal searched for the truth of a place," she wrote, "and I for a metaphor."

After viewing the show, we drove up Boulder Canyon to have dinner at The Red Lion Inn, which sits alone by a creek amid forests of pine trees. Later, as the sun was setting, Carrie, John, and I stood outside, staring at a golden mist that veiled the Rocky Mountains. "Carrie," I said, "it's so beautiful. How can we ever leave Boulder?" She assured me that natural beauty could be found anywhere, "wherever people haven't ruined it."

And then she told us that when Hal was dying, he was very stoic, but she felt his sadness in some of the last words he spoke: "Our world is so beautiful," he said. "How can anyone bear to leave it?"

I sometimes wonder why we're here, all of us, living on this planet. Most likely, there are many reasons. But one of them, I'm sure, is this: to see the beauty, to savor it, and then create our own. That's how Hal lived. And that's how he died.

· · · · · · · · ·

With beauty before me, may I walk.
With beauty behind me, may I walk.

With beauty above me, may I walk.
With beauty below me, may I walk.
With beauty all around me, may I walk.

In old age wandering on a trail of beauty,
lively, may I walk.
In old age wandering on a trail of beauty,
living again, may I walk.
It is finished in beauty.
It is finished in beauty.

— A NAVAJO PRAYER

Part Four

TO FORGIVE
IS DIVINE

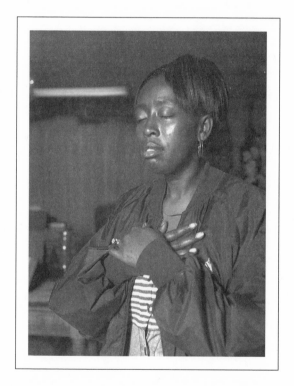

When we forgive, we return to our center,
where things on a good day feel just right.

LOOKING FOR GOD
IN ALL THE WRONG PLACES

I was wrestling with night demons, reliving a fight I'd just had with a friend. In the darkness of the hour, I saw her as cold, scary, and attacking, and myself as hurt, innocent, and ready to strike back. "See God in everyone," I thought, an adage I once read — written by some monk, I bet, who lived in a cave, with no friends or family to deal with.

I mean, seeing God in everyone isn't something I easily do. The first time it happened was in the '70s on the New Jersey Turnpike, when Barry and the kids and I stopped for lunch at a Howard Johnson's.

The kids were cranky and fighting, tired from the long ride. I was cranky, too, muttering about fast-food chains and how there'd be nothing here I'd like and I'd rather starve. The waitress, who had a beehive hairdo and whose name badge said "Pat," smiled broadly and handed us menus.

Well. The special of the day was Key Lime Pie. Now that just happens to be my favorite dessert. Still, I grumbled, it would probably be all chemicals and taste like that too. It's just a stupid "Ho-Jo's," what do you expect? But I took a chance and here's the truth: It was the best key lime pie I ever ate. Cool, tart, and a crust like butter. I savored each bite, and as I did I looked around. What I saw were families: all sizes, all races, laughing and eating, squabbling and alive! A wave of love washed through me, and I suddenly saw God everywhere — in that pie and in Pat and in everyone in the room.

Right. But you can't just make that kind of thing happen. And on this dark, restless night decades later, I sure wasn't seeing God in my angry friend. Forget God. I wasn't even seeing anything *good*.

Then I thought of something the Dalai Lama said, something about remembering the good in the person you're angry at, the things you like.

With that in mind, I began to remember my friend's humor, her empathy, and how she was there for me when I was sick. Soon, she didn't seem so scary or bad. In fact, she began to look again like my friend.

Seeing God in everyone isn't easy. But when you see the good in them, you're halfway there. And the funny thing is, what you see is what you get. You just need to know where to look.

WHAT THE DALAI LAMA SAID

There are few things that feel worse than being angry at someone, and few things feel better than forgiving them. And yet, I sometimes find it hard to forgive — especially when I *know* I'm right. What helps are these words from the Dalai Lama.

When His Holiness came to Boulder, John and I joined 2,000 others to see him and hear him speak. He looked just like his pictures: same bald head and bushy eyebrows, same gold and crimson robes. What surprised us, though, was his laugh — a happy, almost goofy giggle interspersed throughout his talk. It seemed a little odd at first, like, Is this the Dalai Lama? But soon, it seemed transcendent and had me giggling too. And while I've forgotten much of what he said, I'll never forget the brilliance of his smile. We felt he was smiling right at us; most likely others felt the same.

He spoke of many things that day, including forgiveness. But in the end, it was his joyful laugh and radiant smile that made us feel blessed to be in his presence.

A few years later, I found these guidelines for forgiveness offered by the Dalai Lama. I'm not sure where I read them, so it's my words telling his thoughts as best as I recall them. Still, that's how recipes get passed on, right?

THE DALAI LAMA'S RECIPE FOR FORGIVENESS

When you're very angry with someone and having trouble forgiving them, do these three things:

1. Consider why you think the person did what they did that is bothering you. Given all that you know about them, what could have provoked or motivated them to do this? (*Besides the fact that they're one bad dude.*)

2. Recall a time when *you* did something similar. (*This one's disturbingly easy.*)

3. Think of all the good things about this person, the things you like. (*Harder with some folks, but worth a try.*)

Finally, His Holiness reminds us that forgiveness is a gift we give to ourselves. When we're angry, we feel miserable, physically and emotionally. When we forgive, we return to our center, where things on a good day feel just right.

And if you doubt the Dalai Lama, consider this: Research confirms that "forgiveness interventions" are good for the heart, can relieve pain and depression, and enhance the quality of life among the very ill.

It's enough to kill the charge I get from any righteous anger.

A DAY TO REMEMBER

One September, John had a sports-writing assignment
in Salzburg, Austria, and he asked me if I'd come along.
I immediately envisioned *The Sound of Music*, the film that
was made there, where the actual story took place. Sure,
I said, recalling pastoral scenes in which Julie Andrews
ran about singing with a bunch of tow-haired kids. Then
I found out that the week we'd be there included one of
Judaism's holiest days: Rosh Hashanah, the Jewish New
Year and "Day of Remembrance," when we recall what we
did in the year gone by and remember our divine source.
In Boulder, I spend this day alone in the mountains,
praying for forgiveness and forgiving others, because Rosh
Hashanah is also about forgiveness, clearing the way for a
fresh start. But in Austria, I thought, I'd spend the day in
a temple. I went online to search.

What I found was that Salzburg's history included
virulent anti-Semitism — especially in the 1400s
and during the Third Reich — and its once vibrant
community of Jews was now reduced to about 100.
Of course. I had forgotten the dark story beneath *The
Sound of Music*'s jolly songs: a tale of Nazism engulfing a
city and its people. I now felt a responsibility to attend
Salzburg's only remaining synagogue in solidarity. But
I also felt a growing aversion and no longer wanted to
go. I wondered how it would feel on a Jewish Day of Awe

to be in a city once proud to declare itself "*judenfrei*," free of Jews. I worried that I wouldn't open my heart in forgiveness at a time when we're asked to forgive. Which is why, before we left Boulder, I went to a pre-holiday talk led by Rabbi Zalman Schachter-Shalomi, a renowned ecumenist, and his wife, Eve Ilsen.

I really like Reb Zalman. He's the beloved founder of the Jewish Renewal movement. He's also a Hasidic master with a zest for life and a sense of humor that's *heimishe* (the Jewish version of folksy). And Eve, his *rebbetzin*, is a gifted teacher with her own comic flair. So I told them my concerns, and they were deeply empathetic, for Reb Zalman was raised in Vienna and fled from the Nazis in 1939. They advised me to spend most of my time in Salzburg just looking at people and noting what I saw. Try to look without preconceptions, they said. See them as real, as human; see the good and the bad.

It was advice I followed. And what I generally saw were amiable people whose tastes were curiously similar to mine. They love to hike and polka (one of the few dances John and I can do together, galloping across the floor), drink beer and listen to Mozart (good choices both), and eat marzipan (which I love, even when it's brown slabs like we bought in a shop there and polished off at dinner). And they seemed rightfully proud of their golden city with its winding river, whimsical gardens, spires and domes. I also saw some people who seemed cold and aloof, and I learned that many Salzburgers, like many Austrians, were not ready to face the darker side of their past.

On Rosh Hashanah, the iron gates in front of the temple were locked. There were armed, unsmiling policemen on guard, and they asked me in German for my ID, since another synagogue in Austria had recently been bombed. It felt strange and chilling. For a moment, I felt like other Jews must have felt facing Nazis.

But once inside the temple, I began to feel at home. The small congregation seemed happy to have one more congregant, and the Hebrew prayers we sang were the same ones I sang as a child — the same prayers chanted by Jews all over the world for thousands of years — and some even had the same tunes. I also noted that while most people there were friendly, a few seemed ... cold and aloof.

Later, I hiked up the town's small mountain and smiled back at the Austrians descending, who greeted me with a hearty "*Guten morgen!*" There were two I remember still. One was a lost Austrian or German tourist, who held out a map and asked me questions in German. "I speak English, only English," I said, amazed that he thought this dark-eyed Jewess was one of them. The other was a handsome, white-haired man, who looked a little older than I. When we passed each other on the trail, he smiled and stopped to talk. He was a Salzburger, he told me in perfect English, and for a few minutes we walked side-by-side, enjoying each other and the sun-kissed day. I liked him. I sensed his goodness, and he felt familiar.

When I reached the top of the mountain, I sat on the grass, looked down at this beautiful city, and was grateful to see its citizens as people, simply people, human and real. Then I did my rites of forgiveness. And on that Rosh Hashanah in Salzburg, I came to a place of peace.

RITES OF FORGIVENESS

The rites I did on that mountaintop in Salzburg were the
same ones I do each Rosh Hashanah in Boulder, the ones
I learned decades ago from Shakti Gawain.

Shakti's many books include *Creative Visualization,* in
which she teaches ways to transform our lives and our
selves. One exercise she suggests that I never forgot deals
with forgiveness: forgiving others and forgiving yourself.
I've changed and adapted it over the years, but this recipe
comes from Shakti. It's a powerful exercise that can be
very healing. When I'm done, I feel lighter and often find
myself crying. You can do it any time you want or need. I
do it once a year, on Rosh Hashanah.

Before I start, I find a quiet, sheltered place where I
won't be disturbed by people or phones. If it's a nice day, I
like to hike up the foothills, sit under a tree, and begin.

FORGIVING OTHERS

1. Write down the names of anyone, living or dead, who
   hurt you or toward whom you feel anger. Next to each
   name, jot down briefly what he or she did or what
   you're angry about. (Sometimes I skip the writing and
   just start with Step 2.)
2. Close your eyes, relax, and visualize each person you're
   angry with, one at a time. Imagine yourself telling

them why you feel angry or hurt, but adding that you now want to forgive them and clear up your relationship. See how they respond and what they say. Then, if and when you feel ready, look into their eyes and say something like, "I forgive you and bless you. Be happy and go your way." Repeat this process with each person on your list.

3. When no more people come to mind, write down or say, "I forgive you and release you all." Then you can tear up the paper and throw it away. If I'm near a body of water, I drop the bits of paper into it and watch them drift downstream.

It might be hard to forgive some people the first time you do this. But if you continue to do the exercise now and again, things should eventually feel resolved. It helps to remember that this ritual is for your own well-being. Still, it might help heal the other people too.

FORGIVING YOURSELF

The same exercise serves to *ask* for forgiveness. This time you write down (or picture) all the people you have hurt or would like to ask forgiveness from. Then, with your eyes closed, visualize yourself asking each person, one at a time, for forgiveness, hearing what they say, and receiving their blessing and release. When you feel the process is complete, you can affirm, "I forgive myself, now and forever," tear up the paper, and throw it away.

True, forever is a long time. But you can do these rites as often as you need.

Part Five

FRIENDS AND NEIGHBORS, LOVERS AND STRANGERS

The more I learn about our world,
I sense a kindness at its core.
And it seems that all species
instinctively know how to take
care of each other.

DO YOU GIVE TO THE
ONES WHO ARE DRUNK?

My son, Tony, who lives in Manhattan, keeps some change in his pocket when he goes out walking. That way, he has something to give to the people he passes who ask him for help.

"Do you give to the ones who are drunk, who may use it to buy more beer?" I asked.

"Yeah," he said. "It's not for me to judge them or how they'll use it. You give from compassion to people in need."

So now, when I remember, I keep change in my pocket too. It helps me look forward to outstretched hands that I sometimes used to resent.

In Judaism, giving to the needy is considered by some sages to be the most important commandment of all. It's called *tzedakah* — which often translates as "charity" but truly means "righteousness." It's simply doing what is right and just.

Maimonides, a medieval rabbi and philosopher, wrote that there are eight levels of *tzedakah,* and one of the highest is to "give to the poor without knowing to whom one gives and without the recipient knowing from whom he received."

But something special happens when you're face-to-face on the street. It's a chance to really see each other and your shared humanity, and both giver and receiver end up feeling good. I feel especially good if I give with a smile and wish them good luck.

Maimonides also wrote, "Even a poor person who lives entirely on *tzedakah* must give *tzedakah* to another." Which reminds me of our friend Julia Dean.

Julia teaches photography around the world, but this story happened when she was a struggling artist in New York. It was a snowy winter day with a biting wind. Julia still remembers it because she walked home forty blocks in the cold, not having enough money for a bus.

"I was ten blocks from my apartment," she says, "when a man huddled in a doorway held out a can filled with change and said, 'Lady, you got any money?' It hit me that I didn't, I didn't have *any* money, and I started to cry. He looked at me and then held out the can again and said, 'Lady, you need some money?'"

THE BALLAD OF
PAM AND RENATO

Pam and Renato fell in love. It happened in Mexico, where they then built a home, *"Casa de Pamela y Renato."* Each of them came from a troubled past and had lived their share of sadness. Pam was about ten years older than Renato, but their souls were similarly young and old, and they were both, above all, free spirits. Having finally found each other, they felt, well, ecstatic.

It was hard not to feel a little envious around them. Their love and passion were palpable, their joy in life boundless. They did cartwheels and headstands on the nude beach near their village, and took photographs to capture it all. That's what they wanted most: to capture it all. So they made a list of 100 things they would do together before they died. Far-off adventures. Spiritual journeys. Ways to express their love: prosaic things like learning acceptance; and poetic things like studying the Kama Sutra's sixty-four arts of love, which include magic, mimicry, and practice with bow and arrow (along with more erotic pursuits, such as slowly feeding your lover grapes).

The last time we saw them together was when they returned from a year in India, visiting all the places tourists are warned away from and finding gurus who drove taxis on the side. We were in Mexico on vacation, renting a *casa* next to theirs.

Some months later, Pam drove Renato to the Puerto Vallarta airport. He was flying to San Francisco, where he worked as a firefighter. He took the Alaska Airlines flight, the one that crashed into the Pacific Ocean. There were no survivors. He was thirty-nine.

I later wondered how many things on their list they had managed to do before he died. But then I decided it didn't matter. Just making the list together was a blessing of their love.

BUDDIES ON THE PATH

When I was a kid and went to camp, we had a buddy system when we swam in the lake. Every five minutes the lifeguard would blow her whistle, and you would find your buddy, grab her hand tight, and hold your hands up together. It was a way to make sure no one drowned.

Well, it helps to have a buddy on the spiritual path, too, and mine is Ellie. I call her when life seems too dark or too much, and she reminds me of the wisdom that can save me from drowning. We try to meet every Friday at 4, and if we're at Ellie's, we sit on Indian blankets in her Spanish-style home, light candles on the altar, and make room for Tashi, her black labrador mutt.

Sometimes we play music together — Ellie on dulcimer, me on guitar — and then meditate. Sometimes we talk about problems we're having with our family or mate, and then help each other see the other side and act from a higher perspective. And sometimes we pray.

Recently, we skipped a Friday when Ellie and her partner, Annie, went to New Mexico on a Quaker retreat. Before they left, they were wondering: Did they really want to spend their vacation meditating, praying, and discussing their spiritual life in small groups? As opposed to, say, swimming in Cozumel and drinking margaritas?

But the next time we met, Ellie said the retreat was great, just what they needed, individually and as a couple. And it had strengthened her will to maintain a daily practice, now that she saw how good that made her feel.

That said, we lit a candle and sat down for meditation. Ellie set a timer for 20 minutes, and our session began.

My thoughts were scattered — a little this, a little that. Watch your breath, I told myself: in, out.

After more distractions, I tried a mantra: "Hum sa. I am that." Hum (inhale). Sa (exhale). Hum (in). Sa (out).

Then I began planning what I'd make for dinner. Sarah and Paul were coming. Copper River salmon. Yes! And Sarah likes black olives. Lots of black olives.

Don't think about dinner. You're supposed to be meditating.

But the dinner's for Sarah, who's having brain surgery. I felt good doing something nice for Sarah. Then I felt good about being good. Aargh! Spiritual pride!

Hum. Sa. Hum. Sa. HumSaHumSaHumSa.

We'll have spinach with the salmon, fresh spinach simply steamed. And goat cheese and crackers for starters. With drinks. I think I'll have tequila. Yeah, I really want tequila, with lime and salt and that nice floaty feeling. Ahhh.

Rivvy, cut the tequila and watch your breath: in, out, in, out —

And that's when the timer went off. Ellie hit the chime and our meditation was over.

"Oh *amiga*," Ellie said, "I feel so glad. Not just for our friendship and the good times we have, but that we're spiritual buddies too."

"Well," I responded, thinking of my dinner meditation (and some unkind words I had said the day before), "I'm glad I can also tell you when I'm feeling *un*spiritual!"

"Right," she said. "That's part of it." Then she told me about the last day of her retreat. She was sitting with her group for their morning discussion and they were sharing how they felt about going home. Ellie told them she was scared that she wouldn't be able to stay on a spiritual path, but would fall off it and essentially fail.

"And right after I said that, I thought, 'How arrogant,'" Ellie said laughing. "I mean, every saint and yogi falls, so of course I will too. But you know what? I think it's the times I fall that I learn and grow the most. They're a big part of the spiritual path."

"They are?" I asked. I hadn't thought of it that way.

"Yeah," Ellie said. "Maybe that's how you know you're *on* a spiritual path — when you fall off it!"

I took her hand and held it tight. She's my buddy.

ON THE "A" TRAIN

The silver-haired man who smiled at me on the subway was very old and poorly dressed, but wore his age and shabby blazer with elegance. It was a day so steamy hot and humid that people looked at each other more than usual, too wilted to bother looking away. Most of them just stared and sighed, without the energy to even nod.

The old man and I looked at each other in that ener-vated way, and then we looked again and started to smile. I got a slight sense of shining from all the gold in his teeth. I also got an instant jolt of connection.

"That's half the battle," he said. "It's half won when you get one person to smile at you during the day."

"What's the other half?" I asked, still smiling.

"I don't know," he laughed. "I'm not old enough yet."

. . . .

"Sometimes your joy is the source of your smile,
but sometimes your smile can be the source of your joy."
— THICH NHAT HANH

WHAT IS WANTED?
WHAT IS NEEDED?

My mother told me this story about her eighty-something partner, Len.

One night, Mom and Len were at a very nice restaurant enjoying a good dinner. At a table nearby, however, a young couple sat, holding their baby who wouldn't stop crying. So Len finished his dinner and then went over to the crying-baby table.

"Did he reprimand them for bringing a baby to a fancy restaurant and ruining your meal?" I asked, which is something I might have wanted to do but not have had the nerve.

"No," Mom said. "He offered to hold their baby so they could enjoy their dinner."

Wow, I thought. And then I thought of est....

Back in the early 1970s, when some people were trying out all sorts of things, I was one of those people and I tried out "est," the lower-cased acronym for Erhard Seminars Training, founded by Werner Erhard, guru of the human potential movement. est was supposed to help you find "it" — which was not defined and once found is soon lost — and I never knew if I really found "it." I was worried that I was the only one who didn't, but then, maybe others were worried too.

The training became infamous for being led by ex-marines who wouldn't let you leave for the bathroom until the breaks. Well, there were some strange things going on, but some good things, too, and a few lessons I never forgot. One was Werner's advice on how to relate to this world we live in. Simple advice, like a recipe: Look around and ask yourself, What is wanted? What is needed?

I think of that sometimes when I'm in a meeting, or with my children, or feeling restless or self-absorbed. What is wanted? What is needed? Then I go pitch in.

And just in case I'm feeling too proud of my deeds, I'm always humbled when I hear of people who go way beyond what I envision. People like Len, holding that baby.

CONFESSIONS OF
A LISTAHOLIC

I'm addicted to making lists. I make lists of What to Do,
Who to See, What to Research, and Who to Call. And
when my lists get too long, I make lists from my lists:
What to do Today, What to do Soon, What to do in The
Future. I write long lists in yellow tablets and short lists
on index cards. I look over the relevant lists almost daily
and use a highlighter to set priorities.

Yes, I know, over the top. But now and then, the
value of lists becomes clear. You see, before listoma-
nia hit me, I'd often hear that a neighbor was sick, or a
colleague lost a parent, or a friend was getting divorced,
and I'd think, I should send a card, or drop off a meal,
or call and make a date ... but then my life would get too
busy and I'd forget.

So now I write down my intentions as soon as I have
them — send get-well card to Rita; give thank-you gift to
Charlie; visit Katherine — and they're there on a list to
remind me, until I do the deed and cross them off. (And
for list makers, few things are more gratifying than cross-
ing things off!)

Some things stay on my list far too long. Others I
thankfully do just in time. Here's one:

Our neighbor Jack had been very ill for months.
I put his name on one of my lists to remember to pray

for him and call now and then to see if I could help.
One day, the list prompted me to take him something
that might cheer him up, and I had just the thing: a CD
called *Facing Future,* by a Hawaiian singer named Israel
Kamakawiwo'ole. It's so lyrical and uplifting that I
bought a few of them to give to friends. So I took one
over for Jack and left it by the door. Later, his wife, KC,
called to say that Jack had gone into the hospital a week
before to have a stem cell transplant. The chemotherapy
was making it hard for him to talk or read, she said, but
the one thing that made him feel better was listening to
music.

Thank you, list. Much obliged.

A ONE-MINUTE RECIPE FROM MEXICO

We were on vacation in a small Mexican village. Gwen, a friend we first met there, was staying in another small village nearby. So we arranged for her to spend her last night with us.

She arrived in a white taxi and stepped out holding her bag. John and I ran to greet her. Then the taxi driver got out and walked toward us, offering his hand. "Juan," he said with a big warm smile. We all shook hands. I thought he would say more or give us his card, but that was it, and he drove away.

That's when Gwen told us she had kept the driver waiting twenty minutes when he picked her up.

"I apologized to him several times," she said. "He was nervous because he had another pickup to do right after me."

She paused and then added, "What a nice man. He was worried and rushed, yet he still took time to meet you, a minute to connect."

YOUNG BABES AND OLD BROADS

Most of us spend time with people our age. Here's what can happen when you don't.

YOUNG BABES

It was Christmas week, which explained it: John and I were stuck for hours in an endless line at customs in Gatwick Airport, London. We were lost in a mass of families, most of them Muslim. The women were wearing black or white hijabs, scarves that covered their hair and neck, and holding onto their children, who looked tired and cranky. I was feeling the same — and also nervous, since this was the year of the shoe bomber and other plots by Islamic extremists. In fact, I was about to succumb to a very dark mood when I spotted in front of us a little Pakistani boy propped on his mother's back and crying. He looked about two years old and was surrounded by family members; but none were paying him attention as they, too, looked ready to cry.

So I stepped into my best routine: hiding. I ducked behind John's back and then popped my head above his right shoulder with a big smile and a "boo!" Then I hid again, this time appearing above John's left shoulder. Well, I got the baby's attention, and before long he stopped crying. In fact, he started to smile and soon was chortling. Cool, I thought, we're playing peek-a-boo in Pakistani! Then his young mother turned around, and she smiled too. She spoke to others who were with her, and they nodded at me as I nodded back. In that moment, in that interminable line at that crowded airport, I felt happy: connected to a whole group of people I had stopped seeing as "family" and to this sweet baby boy who helped make me see.

HUM

One winter, John went to Africa, to a rural village in Mali. A European company was celebrating its centennial there by helping the villagers plant trees — one million trees — and John was invited to cover the story.

To launch the project, there was an outdoor ceremony near the pond, and every tribal chief and elder was present. After listening to four chiefs speak, and spotting five others lined up to follow, John drifted away to view a mud-built, castle-like mosque, near the arc of huts where most people lived.

Soon after he started walking, John felt something warm and gentle in his hand. Looking down, he saw a young, barefoot boy, who held tightly onto his hand and smiled. John pointed to himself and said "John." Then he pointed to the little boy, who said "Hum." And for the next two hours, wherever John went, Hum went, never letting go of his hand. They wandered through the village, into the school, and even planted a tree together and named it "Hum John."

"He had such trust," John later told me. "I think it's because of the village. It felt so open and safe, as if all the adults were there for all the children." I remembered the African saying, "It takes a village to raise a child."

John was moved by the warmth of the Mali people, by their music and their easy smiles. But what he'll never forget is Hum, the little boy who took his hand.

TWENTY-SOMETHING

Another good thing about mixing the ages is it keeps you in tune with the changing times and expressions. I had a twenty-something guitar teacher named Dylan, who would always say to me, "No worries." Whenever I changed our appointment, whenever I forgot what he taught me, whenever I did anything wrong, that's what he said: "No worries."

It's a kind phrase, I think, and reassuring. It makes me feel good about this new generation.

"But Dylan," I told him one day, "I'm Jewish, I worry!"

He smiled at me and said, "No worries."

And now I'm saying it too.

VISITING OUR ELDERS

Visiting our elders is a *mitzvah* (see *"Mitzvah"* recipe). It's one of those things I feel I'm meant to do, and it's what I hope others will feel *they're* meant to do when I'm older. It's also, almost always, a source of joy: There's the joy you give them, and the joy you feel seeing their joy, and the joy they give *you* with their stories and inspiration.

Now, some elders are more fun than others. So it goes. Katherine, a ninety-something neighbor, wasn't a great talker, which meant it was sometimes a strain to keep the conversation going. If I asked her what was happening, she usually told me about her back pain.

Not a great topic. But we all need someone to complain to, right? So I would take off my sweater and listen.

The reason I took off my sweater was because Katherine, like many older people, kept the thermostat at about 85 degrees, winter and summer, which made her house warm as Miami and also made me sleepy. But she was my next-door neighbor, so I tried to visit once a week. I mean, imagine what it's like to live alone when you're old and don't get out much or have many friends still alive, so you just sit there, most of the time, watching television. You'd welcome some company, no?

Whenever I'd visit, Katherine would give a surprised "Oh, hi" and a smile. Then she'd sit back down in a grey reclining chair, and I'd sit in a brown leather chair facing her. Slowly, our relationship evolved. We even found things to talk about — things we liked doing as kids, politics, and Oprah.

One day Katherine told me how she was raised: by elderly adoptive parents in the Midwest who believed that children were meant to be silent and just listen. Well, no wonder she wasn't much of a talker! Shortly after that, I stopped worrying about keeping the conversation going. In fact, one day, when I was tired and her house was even warmer than usual, I sat in that brown leather chair, closed my eyes, and fell asleep. I must have slept for ten minutes, and when I woke up, Katherine was still sitting facing me, and it was all okay. How nice it felt to be with someone and it was fine to just be there, to even fall asleep. When I left, she said, as always, "Thanks for coming. It means a lot to me."

Joy.

AND THEN THERE WAS RITA

And then there was Rita. Irish Rita from the Bronx.
White hair in a bob, impish green eyes, a tough little
woman with a big spirit. She was my friend Paul V.'s
mother and the most fun elder I ever met, bar none.

Rita was earthy. She'd tell bawdy jokes and was a
great storyteller, imitating the voices of everyone she
described. And whenever John was coming back from a
business trip, she'd urge me to "make whoopee! Make *lots*
of whoopee! Do it for me!"

A devout if irreverent Catholic, Rita's conversations
were sprinkled with casual references to The Blessed
Mother, The Mother of the Whole World, whom I came to
envision as a female version of The Great Spirit. "Rivvy,"
Rita kindly assured me, "she's the Mother of *All*. That
means Catholics and *Jews* and everyone."

Rita prayed a lot, for anyone in need, and she
strongly believed that her prayers would be heard. "She's
got a direct line to heaven," our friend Helen con-
firmed. So whenever I was sick or scared or someone
in my family had a problem, I asked Rita to pray for
us. Later, she'd tell me how she wrote out the names I
gave her and put them by the small statue of the Blessed
Mother she kept on her bedroom bureau. Once I knew
that, I felt better.

When Rita reached her nineties, her health faded.
Small strokes and a few falls left her needing a walker
and mostly stuck in her apartment. So John and I would
visit her there and take Chinese food, her favorite.
"Chicken with nuts," she'd order, "and brown rice, not
white." She would always have lots of cake, chocolates,

and tea waiting for us, and while we ate she'd tell her stories and we'd all laugh. She especially loved telling us that she was born in Fall River, Massachusetts, home of the infamous accused murderer Lizzie Borden. Rita would get this devilish look on her face as she recited with glee, "Lizzie Borden had an ax, she gave her mother forty whacks; when she saw what she had done, she gave her father forty-one!"

One day, Jeanne V. called to say Rita's health had worsened. They were moving her to assisted living. "She can't live alone anymore," Jeanne explained. "Yesterday, she lost the feeling in her legs and couldn't get up from the bathtub. So she lay there for hours before using her beeper to call *anyone*. I think she's lost her judgment. She's better off where she's going."

John and I made plans to go see her, but we were a little scared — afraid she'd be depressed about leaving her home, and not sure how she'd seem without her "judgment."

"It's a big change," Rita told me on the phone, "a big change."

When we arrived at her new place, she looked smaller than before, even though she was now in a much smaller space: one room, in which Paul and Jeanne had neatly placed her bed and bureau, one chair, the statue of The Blessed Mother, and pictures on the wall.

"Sit in the chair," Rita insisted, as she sat down next to John on the bed. Then she asked him to open the bottom drawer of her bureau — and damn if she didn't have a cache of chocolates there, too, which the three of us began to munch. Soon, Rita was chatting it up like old times, imitating the physical therapist who would bark at her, "Knees! Toes! Knees!" and telling us about the nurse she liked best, Rosie Vasquez, who had a bad neck, so Rita gave her a massage.

We asked how her legs were doing, and she told us the story of being stuck in the tub. "But why did you wait so long to use your beeper?" I asked. "Because I didn't want some *firemen* breaking in and seeing me *naked,*" Rita explained.

"Stupid me," she laughed, "being modest! Wouldn't you know, the day I got here they had this big, burly man give me a shower. He was really *big* (Rita put her hands out to show just how big he was) and he washed me *all over.* Then he dried me down with a towel and puffs of air. Poof, poof." Rita laughed and laughed, saying, "Oh God! Let me tell you! Poof here. Poof there. Well, I figured, I'm this bag of bones and he's probably seen everything, so why not? And there I was worried about some firemen seeing me naked!"

Right before we left, I noticed something pinned to her wall — a simple white cloth with red embroidered words: "Sparkle with the Spirit."

"The nuns gave it to me," Rita said.

They gave it to the right person.

JUST LIKE ME

It was one week after Annie's birthday, and we had invited her and Ellie to dinner. Just as we sat down to eat, the doorbell rang. Since it was a wintry Sunday evening, I was curious as to whom it could be. When I opened the door, I felt the darkness and the cold. A man in his thirties was standing there, holding a clipboard.

"We're in the middle of a party," I said, with a dollop of self-righteous anger. Then I felt bad. He probably just needed me to sign some petition — to clean the rivers, or save the prairie dogs, or some such Boulder thing. So in a kinder tone, I asked, "What do you want?"

"Do you need any patio glass or door panels?" he said, and my anger revved up again. How rude to knock on our door on a Sunday night to try and *sell* something. "No," I said in my original tone. "Good night."

Back at the table, I relayed what had happened. "Poor guy," Annie said. "He must be really hard off to go out on a night like this." Ellie muttered something about how this recession was hitting everyone. And guilt whisked in to replace my anger.

"You're so much more compassionate than I am," I said.

Ellie laughed. "Well, we've been practicing it lately," she said, "using Buddhist teachings."

"We read something out loud every day," Annie said, "from our favorite teachers."

Sensing that my own compassion needed a lift, I asked them to cut to the chase. So they offered me this guidance that came from Pema Chödrön, the beloved Buddhist nun who brings it all back home.

"With everyone you meet and every encounter," Annie said, "you can say to yourself, 'Just like me.' Especially if you're feeling judgmental. So with that guy you just met, you could look and say, 'He's trying to make a living best he can … just like me.' Or, 'He needs money … just like me.' Or, 'He's self-focused … just like me.'"

I like this. It's simple, it's basic, and it works: Buddhism for Dummies — just like me.

. . . .

Nasrudin walked into a bank. The teller asked
if he could identify himself. Nasrudin took out a mirror,
looked into it, and said, "Yep. That's me!"

— A SUFI STORY

SERVING (PEOPLE) (DINNER)

One nearly freezing Christmas Eve, John and I volunteered to help serve dinner to the homeless at a restaurant in downtown Boulder. I was a little nervous, afraid we'd seem condescending, or that the people we'd be serving would be depressed, crazy, or angry, or that I'd be my usual klutzy self and spill cranberry sauce all over their laps. But it turned out not to be that way at all.

The place was festively decorated with silver garlands and red poinsettias. Christmas songs were playing over the loudspeakers, and the excitement shown by our guests inspired me to be the very best waitress I could possibly be. "Would you like more coffee, sir?" "Is everything okay, ma'am?"

Some of the people looked truly impoverished, just wearing thin sweaters on this very cold night. Others looked like old hippies, not that different from our friends or us (a thought both comforting and disconcerting). And while many were elders, there were also young families holding babies on their laps.

One woman seemed disgruntled and complained that her roll was hard — which it was, so I got her another. And one man made it clear that I was being overly solicitous — which I was, so I toned it down. But the main feeling was joy, simple joy: among the homeless, among the servers, and among the kitchen help (including John), who were cooking green beans and yams and filling plates with abundance.

Rushing from the kitchen to the tables to give everyone their turkey dinner and seeing their smiles widen as they received it — "More gravy?" "Oh yes!" — made me want to spend my whole life doing just that.

It also made me see that under all the details of our lives, we are always just learning to serve each other, no matter what we do. To practice it this simply was a lesson, and a gift.

HAVE A GREAT DAY! *NOT.*

When I'm in a mood and people tell me, "Have a great day!" I want to mutter, "What's wrong with a *nice* day or a *fair* day? Why do I have to have a *great* day, grumble, grumble...." This "great day" greeting is rampant in Boulder markets, most often heard at checkout.

But one day at Whole Foods, a cool young guy stacking the shelves helped me find rice cakes and said, in parting, "Have a grateful day!" Whoa, that stopped me. Have a *grateful* day.

Some people say that gratefulness is the key to a sacred life. Others say it's the key to happiness. There have even been studies that correlate gratitude with good health, less depression, and a good night's sleep. Well, yeah. But how do you have a grateful day?

I think it starts by saying "thank you." And when I begin each morning with these words, it helps set the tone (at the least, it mollifies my morning blues). It could be as simple as giving thanks for another day or the sound of the morning rain.

To expand my gratitude, I might follow the lead of Dr. Michael Beckwith, "the Rev" and founder of the Agape International Spiritual Center. He suggests picking one day now and then when you find something to be thankful for every hour — and express it. I tried this and was surprised that just by having the intention, I actually remembered to do it. Every hour, more or less, I looked around or within, found something to be thankful for, and said it: "Thank you for this peaceful day" "Thank you, blackbird, for that lovely song" "Thank you, John, for mowing the lawn."

Since then, whenever I feel a swelling of gratitude or appreciation, I often say it out loud. Sometimes I say it right to the source: "Thank you, trees!" "Thank you, sunshine!" And sometimes I go to the source beyond: "Thank you, Great Spirit, for all this beauty!" "Thank you, Lord, for helping Mom get better."

It also helps, I find, to spread my thanks around, even to those anonymous ones who offer tech support on the phone.

"Thank you so much," I said to the man in Sri Lanka who helped me reconnect to the Web. "That was really helpful. You told me what to do in ways I could understand." And when he responded, "I'm happy to be of service," I felt like I was in a Jimmy Stewart movie from the '40s, and I hung up feeling good.

In fact, the more I say thank you, the better I feel, so I say it whenever I feel it. If I look up at the mountains and spontaneously say, "Omigod, it's so beautiful," I remember to add, "Thank you!" Or I'll be out to dinner with friends and feeling so happy in the moment that I'll silently pray, "Thank you for this food, these friends, and this wonderful life."

The whole world is sacred, and we connect with that sacredness when we give thanks.

So have a grateful day. Better yet, have a grateful life.

. . . .

How we suddenly are reminded
that we pass this way but once,
and are expected to give thanks
as best we can.

— STAN GROTEGUT

A GOOD NEIGHBOR

"Hi, Neighbor!"

That's how Jack would greet us, from the first day he moved in. If we saw each other over the backyard fence or passed each other on the street, he'd always say, "Hi, Neighbor!" with a cheerful voice and a big smile. It made me feel good to hear him, and to see him too. Jack was handsome, lanky, and looked like a cowboy.

My mother often said that if everyone just took care of their own little corner, this world would be a wonderful place. I thought of that when Jack died. He was only fifty-three, but he left a big corner behind, and he took care of it all right.

KC, his wife, held a memorial service in their yard: a glorious labyrinth of brick paths and gardens, playgrounds and artistry — all created by Jack, with the help of KC, their family, and friends. Many people spoke at the service, and they told of Jack's kindness and generosity, his work ethic and zest for life. Some spoke of great meals or great fishing trips they shared with him. And I spoke of what he taught John and me about being a good neighbor.

It's a funny thing about neighbors. You might get to see and hear them more than anyone else in your life. And if you're lucky, like we were, you learn from them too.

Truth is, I was kind of envious of Jack. He seemed so happy, so giving and alive, that it was easy to feel like a dark blob beside him. But the good thing about envy is, it points you where you want to go.

Sometimes on weekends, around 7 a.m., we'd hear noise outside, and I'd ask John, What's that? "It's Farmer Jack," he'd say, "working in his garden." Well. We'd soon get up out of bed and start working in ours. And as we watched Jack create wondrous things in his yard, we started fixing up our own. Put rose bushes in places we had previously ignored and planted more vegetables.

Jack would often drop by, offering bags of his new potatoes. The most delicious potatoes we ever ate. And when he'd create objects of beauty, such as exotic birdhouses, he'd carve a design on their back side as well, so we'd see beauty too.

KC and Jack and John and I started having grand-children around the same time, one after the other. We'd hear them playing joyfully with their grandkids, and we watched them build a playhouse, sandbox, and swing. Hmm, we thought, maybe our grandkids would have fun in a tent.

Whenever Jack and I were both working in our yards, he would give that big shining smile, say "Hi, Neighbor!" and stop to talk. We'd chat about vegetables and life. I'd ask him for practical advice. He seemed to know how to do everything. And he'd ask me to recommend the most ro-mantic places I knew, for him to take KC to on her birth-day. Once, when I complained about the hot summer, Jack taught me about whole-house fans, helped us find one, and insisted on installing it himself. That was Jack.

The last time we saw him, just a while before he died, Jack was busy planning, and living, and talking excitedly about a boating trip ahead — despite being debilitated by cancer and the drugs he took to fight it.

So what did we learn from Jack? To enjoy. Be generous. Grow vegetables. Work hard. Create beauty. Be romantic. Have adventures. Love your family. Help your neighbors. And strive to be the brightest, most vibrant spirit you can be.

I said that Jack taught us how to be a good neighbor. But really, he taught us how to live.

. . . .

Recipe inspired by Jack Rietveld,
December 7, 1953 — May 24, 2007

"_ _ _ _ IS CLOSER THAN YOU THINK"

Back in the days when I would get stoned, I liked to get
stoned with Norma and David. Norma would bake these
amazing chocolate prune cakes, which we'd consume in
two minutes once we were high. And David, now and
then, would utter something profound. Of course, when
I was stoned, everything seemed profound. "It's raining
out," someone would say, and I'd go "Wow!"

Well, one stoned night, David proclaimed that everyone in their lifetime gets the same amount of pain, but
some people get it in one lump sum, while others get
fragments spread out through their years. "Wow!" I said.
"That's profound." I wasn't sure if it were true, but I
learned, soon enough, that we each have our cross to bear.

My cross is anxiety, deep anxiety, and, worst of all,
panic attacks. They first appeared in my thirties at a time
of transition, when things seemed unknown, overwhelm-
ing, and dark. My marriage and family had broken up,
and I had just signed up to go back to school. When the
first attack hit me, I was on the subway at Times Square,
and I feared my heart would burst or I was losing my
mind. It felt that way each time it struck — at its worst,
like most things, in the middle of the night.

I tried to befriend it, as some Buddhists advise, but
for me, anxiety was no friend. The friends I did find,
most gratefully, were prayer ("Dear God, please help me

be okay"), and Ativan (anxiety pills), and sometimes both ("Thank you, God, for giving us Ativan"). I also found, as so many have, that the depth of your pain can deepen your journey, your connection to others and to something beyond.

The panic attacks eventually stopped, the anxiety diminished, and the fear became fear about fear. Yet it's always there like a hidden wound that can take me by surprise. Which it did, years later, at a dance class in Boulder.

John was away working in Europe; my mind was adrift in worries; and bad dreams had left me ungrounded. To make things worse, it was a drop-in class, and no one I knew had dropped in. I looked around but found no smiles and remembered words my friend Karen once said: "There's something strange about strangers, you know?" So, there I was, heart beating faster, pins and needles up my back, and surrounded by strangers.

Then I noticed some writing on the whiteboard on the wall. With a light-blue marker, someone had drawn the Hindu symbol for *Om* and written: "_ _ _ _ *is closer than you think.*" The first word was too faded to read. It looked like it had four letters, but no, I thought, it must be "God." "*God is closer than you think.*" A message, perhaps, to assure me: Nothing to be scared of; God is here. I looked around the class again, and this time a young woman with spiky pink hair gave me a big smile. Yes, I thought, God is here and in everyone, even strangers.

Back in that darkest time of my life, I often leaned on the kindness of strangers, and I learned two things. First, most strangers really *are* kind ("Are you all right,

Miss?"). And when I in turn was kind to strangers ("Can I help you carry that?"), the shadow around me would momentarily lift, and I'd remember again that I once knew joy.

At the end of class, I walked up to the whiteboard to read the message more closely. The first word was half-erased, but it clearly had four letters, began with "L," and appeared to be *Love*.

"*Love is closer than you think.*"

There are many names of God, perhaps thousands. The one I like best is Love.

COME, COME, COME TO THE FAIR

Street fairs ... Fiestas ... County fairs ... Parades....
Events so full of life they almost seem transcendent.
Perhaps that's why so many saints' days are celebrated
in Mexico. It's hard to visit a village there without some
festival occurring. "*Señora*," a man in Sayulita once told
me, "this is what life is about — *musica*, dancing, *familia,*
and friends!" Maybe he's right.

What strikes me most at these gatherings is how
nearly everyone looks happy. The streets overflow with
families and food, music and lights, and all kinds of
people wearing all kinds of clothes: cowboy hats, tie-dye,
fairy costumes, and beaded jeans. I walk around dazzled
by the energy and find myself smiling at strangers — and
they're smiling back.

When my kids were young and we lived in Manhattan,
I took them to street fairs on 94th Street or Columbus, and
our excitement would build when we heard the music a
block away. Once there, they would run to the amusement
rides, and I would run to sample the hot tamales, Chinese
dumplings, and funnel cakes with sugar: a United Nations
of food! We paid gypsy-hippies to paint our faces with
stars, and there was magic in the air.

I especially enjoy these gala events if I'm traveling through another state or country. In Salzburg, at
St. Rupert's Fair, I sat with locals at a picnic table, drank

Austrian beer, and soon we were chatting together as we watched young children ride an old-fashioned, hand-painted carousel that used *real* horses — imagine! And at a *carnaval* in Mexico, John and I once dared to ride the junior roller coaster. We were the only adults on it, and we screamed the loudest and got the sickest. All the parents watching were laughing at us, but in a friendly, *simpatico* way. It made me see one truth so clearly: Participation is your ticket to life.

Then there are parades, which I used to look down on. Passive watching, I thought, no interaction. I considered them boring, only to be endured on Thanksgiving for the sake of the kids. Until one summer morning, when beau George took me to a Puerto Rican Day parade on Fifth Avenue. We stood right against the rope, so close we could see the sweat on the men as they played their Latin songs on trumpets and horns. Then high-school marching bands came marching up the street: drummers drumming, young girls waving their native flag, women dancing in long pink and green folk skirts. So much beauty in their brown faces and Spanish eyes. So much pride in who they were. So much noise!

"Kind of wakes you up, doesn't it?" George asked. And I knew he meant all of it, not just the noise.

Street fairs ... Fiestas ... County fairs ... Parades! These are sacred community events. And you're invited.

SOMETHING ABOUT ANGELS

One of the pleasures of staying at a friend's summer house is choosing a book from their well-leafed favorites. Peering into the bookcase at Barry and Tina's Long Island farm, I found a bevy of alluring titles. Then I spotted *Patchwork Planet,* by Anne Tyler, and took it with me to read at my favorite beach.

It's a little beach on the Peconic Bay, and it feels old-fashioned. There are no frills other than a teenage lifeguard. The waves are gentle enough that children play in the sand by the water. And nearly all the women there are stout and wear skirted bathing suits (I think they're mostly Polish, and I'm grateful for their presence. They allow me to stop holding in my stomach, which I generally do in a swimsuit).

Well, I thought, this is heaven: sitting on a beach, letting out my stomach, and reading a book by Anne Tyler. I cherish her books. I even think they're sacred — in the way she showers all her characters with an almost divine compassion, despite or because of their many quirks and flaws.

Patchwork Planet is about Barnaby Gaitlin, who is waiting to meet his personal angel. It's a family tradition, he says. It started with his granddad, who one day met a tall, golden-haired stranger in a grocery store. Her seemingly random words inspired him to find his way and fortune.

I put the book down to take a swim. Floating on my back to look at clouds John said were cirrus, I considered if deep down, everyone believes in angels, or *wants* to believe in angels, or more importantly, wants to meet theirs. I'd like to meet *my* angel, I thought (wondering if I already had, and it was John). And then this thought just came to me: Maybe *I* could be the angel for someone else.

I liked that idea. In fact, I think that's how it works. We all get to be angels for each other, just by saying the right thing at the right time with the right humor or wisdom. It might be as simple as giving a touch, a hug, or a smile. All we have to do is really listen to people, even those we briefly encounter, and respond openly from our heart. We might never know we were their angel, but we could change their lives.

The funny thing is, when I've taken the time to stop and help strangers, they've almost always said in parting, "God bless you," and looked at me in a way that made me feel warm and blessed indeed. Perhaps I wasn't their angel after all, but they were mine.

RECIPES FOR PARTNERS:
KEEPING LOVE SACRED

The love you share with your partner is like electricity. When it's on, you feel a heightened connection to the world and to spirit. When it's off and you want to feel it again, you need to first regain your connection to spirit or your higher self. For me, one way back is through prayer or meditation. I pray to see with eyes of love, to forgive and stop judging. Or, in meditation, I'll notice my anger and hurt and let them pass (letting them pass is the hard part, but it's helpful just to notice).

My mother always said you have to work at a relationship (she especially said it after my divorce). I never liked the sound of that, but alas, it's true. It's a practice to keep love on a higher plane. Here are some ways to return to that space when you find you're on a descent.

When wondering, "Why did I *ever* pick this partner?" that's a good time to remember just why you did: all the things you first loved and admired about them and still love the most. It helps to write these down when you're feeling very loving — to reread when you're not! This is especially useful for people like me, who tend to forget all the good when the bad times come. Oh right, I think, when I read in my list, *"John's a very accepting person who always forgives me."* Hmm, I guess I could give him a *little* slack.

Go to spiritual events together — retreats, chanting, or a talk by a respected teacher, especially one with a good sense of humor — say, Deepak Chopra. I had no idea how funny this man would be in person since his books are rather ponderous. Yet there he was telling how he and his brother ritually scattered their father's ashes in the Ganges River and then joking about where he might scatter his brother's ashes in the future. At his favorite golf course? Or perhaps give them to his nephew so he could finally have his dad in the palm of his hand.... But Deepak wasn't just funny. His talk lifted us into the realm of higher consciousness and back. It was a cosmic trip that we took together, and like all good trips, it deepened our connection.

Here's something we do if we're feeling distant or had a fight and want to get closer. It seems to work best while walking or hiking. We alternate saying things we like or appreciate about each other (with pregnant pauses in between, depending on how far apart we're feeling). It might start like this:

"I like your voice."

"I like how you are with my family."

"I like walking with you."

"I appreciate your willingness to do this."

On a long walk, you have time to remember many things, enough to bring you back.

Sometimes it's enough just to walk together, to see things and feel the wind or sun. It helps change your energy, especially at dawn or dusk, or on warm nights under the stars. If you're angry, you can talk it through or walk in silence. Either way, it works. There's something about walking, step by step, that releases your tension into the air.

Think of your love as a cabbage or rose. I once walked with Ellie through her garden while we discussed the challenges of relationships, specifically our own. "The great thing about gardening," Ellie said, "is that you cultivate the good. Sometimes you get rid of weeds, but mostly, you cultivate the good. Well, that's what we need to do with our partners. Focus on the good. And just looking for it will help bring it out."

Okay, I saved the best for last. This is my all-time favorite recipe for couples. John and I have followed it for years, and it adds sacredness to our life and love. We do it in bed every night, and it starts with gratefulness. Taking turns, back and forth, we say everything we were grateful for that day — the sunshine returning, good news about Mom's health, work we got done, whatever. When that feels complete, we move on to part two, where we share *Something I loved about you today* … or *I loved you most today when* …. It can be something really small, especially on days when you're feeling grim and unloving. But the rule is, you have to say something.

One night, after a morning row that left us barely speaking, just when I thought there was *nothing* I loved about John that day or maybe ever, he said, "I loved you when I heard you laughing on the phone with your sister" — and I smiled and loved him most for that.

EVERYTHING I KNOW
ABOUT SACRED SEX

I took est with Werner Erhard in the '70s, partly because I wanted to raise my consciousness — something the training seemed to promise — and partly because Barry, my estranged husband, had taken it. God forbid his consciousness should be higher than mine!

The sixty-hour course took place on two weekends, and enlightenment aside, the part I was looking forward to most was when Werner would talk about sex. "He tells you all you need to know," Barry told me, refusing to say more.

When the time came, Werner walked to the microphone and announced, "When you're hot, you're hot, and when you're not, you're not." So ended his session on sex.

I feel like that now, writing about sacred sex. When you make love from your heart, sex is sacred. The rest is all details.

FOR THOSE WHO LIKE DETAILS

My friend Gail, who wears sexy costumes on Halloween and other occasions, says the best way to make up with your partner is to make love. That's right. Even when you're fuming with anger and feel anything but love, there's something about making love that does just that: It can bring you closer, higher, and back together.

Why? Because sex is spiritual — powerful and transcendent — and can strengthen your connection to each
other and the divine. Ascetics abstain from sex not because
it's profane, but because it's so sacred. They want to make
love with God and cut out the middleman.

That said, with sacred sex, less could be more.
There's a practice of Orthodox Jews called the Laws of
Family Purity. Derived from biblical commandments,
these laws require couples to cease having sex during a
woman's menstrual period and for one week after. Then,
before again making love, the woman goes to ritual baths
called a *mikvah* and immerses herself in natural waters.

A *mikvah* is a spiritual tool, not a physical one. The
user must be totally clean before immersion and emerges
feeling innocent and renewed. When a woman performs
this ritual after menstruation, she says a prayer, asking
God to sanctify her marriage and her return to intimacy.

I used to think that this practice reflected negative
feelings about women. I now see its intention to make sex
sacred: special and reverent. Judaism, an earthy religion,
regards sex as holy, a gift from God.

But nowhere is sex more revered than in Tantra, a
mystical path to Nirvana. Founded on the belief that all
is one but divided into polarities, Tantra teaches how to
awaken our "Shakti," our deepest, most powerful energy,
as a way to achieve union within, without, and with the
divine. Tantra is a way of life, but it's most known in the
West for the practice of tantric sex, one of many ways to
reach this state of bliss.

John and I were introduced to Tantra in Mexico by a
California-born woman named Pam. A body healer and

teacher of tantric sex, Pam looked the part: Tall, strong, and tanned, she seemed happiest when skinny-dipping or camping out in the jungle.

Tantra, an ancient tradition, evolved in Hinduism and Buddhism and has roots in Asian countries. But there was something about Mexico that made it perfect for our studies. On hot, sultry afternoons, we sat on Pam's vine-covered porch, surrounded by the sweet scent of tropical flowers and the salty smell of the ocean, as she showed us exotic drawings and read from esoteric books. In her candlelit room, she led us through meditations and exercises that used the breath, sounds, vibrations, and visualizations to channel our sexual-heart energy. "It's a way to merge," Pam said, "with each other and the universe. It's called the art of conscious loving."

We soon discovered that tantric sex can ignite amazing energy and ecstatic lovemaking, and we saw how it could be a sacred ritual for self-transcendence. We also discovered that it's a path, and like all paths, it takes study, practice, and commitment. Perhaps because of that, or perhaps because we like spontaneity even more than ritual, back home we resumed our simpler, down-home loving.

Still, some things Pam taught us we now and then do. We might lie spoon-fashion and breathe in sync. Or call each other "beloved." Or make our bedroom a temple of love by lighting candles, playing music, and reading poetry aloud in bed.

But in the end, it comes down to this: When you make love from your heart, sex is sacred. The rest is all details.

TAKE CARE OF EACH OTHER

The more I learn about our world, I sense a kindness at
its core. And it seems that all species instinctively know
how to take care of each other.

One spring morning, Paul and Sarah drove John
and me to a hospital in Denver where John was to have
surgery. Sarah and I sat in the back seat chatting, and I
was looking out the window at all the ranches on the way.
At one ranch, I spotted a herd of cows with their young
calves. It was April, so many babies had just been born.

"Look!" I exclaimed and pointed them out to Sarah.

"Do you know about cow nurseries?" she asked.

"No," I said, and got ready for one of her wonderful
facts. Sarah used to teach immigrant children, so she's
my source of basic knowledge.

"The way it works," she said, "is the cows gather all
the calves in a group, with one cow in charge to watch
over them. And the mother cows take turns being the
caretaker. Look sometime when you see all the babies
together."

I could picture her telling her nine-year-old students
this and how they'd go, "Ohhh, that's nice!"

Well, I said it too: "Ohhh, Sarah, that's nice!"

It helped put me in a good mood for the hospital. Of
course, what really helped was sharing the ride with Paul

and Sarah, our dear buddies, who kept us laughing and talking all the way there.

By the time we arrived, I felt calm, even jolly. As we walked through the corridors, I asked directions to this or that and smiled and thanked everyone in my best possible way. And each nurse who helped John was so helpful and friendly that I believed what Sarah says: Most nurses are angels.

"I feel so relaxed," I said to John.

"I'm glad *you're* relaxed," John the patient said. But he was too. Enough to sing me a song as he lay on the table before being wheeled in to surgery. It was a song about oysters:

> *"Let there be you,*
> *Let there be me.*
> *Let there be oysters*
> *Under the sea.*
>
> *Let there be cuckoos,*
> *A lark and a dove,*
> *But first of all, please …*
> *Let there be love."*

Part Six

A NATURE RECIPE FROM FRANK LLOYD WRIGHT

"Study nature,
Love nature,
Stay close to nature,
It will never fail you."

— FRANK LLOYD WRIGHT

STUDY NATURE

In one of many mid-life transitions, I decided to become a teacher for inner-city kids. So I enrolled at Bank Street College, where we were taught to study nature the way we'd teach our students: not by reading, but observing and reflecting. Watch something as it grows or changes, my professor said, like a plant or the moon. I chose the moon. Journal in hand, off I went, moon hunting.

It's not always easy to find the moon in Manhattan, but for one month, from the same location, I drew where it was at noon and at different hours in the day and night. I sketched its rise and fall and changing shape, and though I never really fathomed what it all meant, I began to suspect that the earth is indeed moving. Then, one night, I woke up from a dream with a visceral sense of our spinning earth, the circling moon, and their amazing, enduring connection. For one moment, I got it, and it was a moment of joy.

I later saw that joy reflected in my third-grade students when they, too, were led to observe and discover. "Look, Miss Rivvy!" Kalima shouted. "Our bean seed is sprouting!" And at the end of the term, they created an album of notes to help me make my next transition: moving to Boulder to live with John. ("Thank you Miss Rivvy for all the good times. I hope you have a nice time with your new life. Love, Willy.")

Once ensconced in Boulder, I entered that expansive space you sometimes enter when you're somewhere new. This led me to attend events I would normally ignore and to join groups I would normally not join — such as The Bioregional Study Group, whose goal was to study our hometown's ecology and learn how to live sustainably within it. We talked about things like compost, which to me seemed exotic, and I soon made two friends, Alison and Milan, who inspired me with their projects. The one I liked best was this:

Milan cut out a huge circle of white poster board and taped it to their kitchen wall. They divided the wheel into twelve months, and as the year progressed, they wrote down under each month all the changes they observed: which star was brightest and where it appeared, when they heard the first mourning dove or found violets in spring. They were creating their own almanac, and, like the Native Americans, they named each month's full moon to track the seasons, with names like *Wet Snow Moon* or *Moon of the Ripe Tomatoes.*

But sometimes, the changes we observe can be disturbing. One summer I noted the absence of honeybees and read that parasitic mites were decimating their species. I missed seeing them and worried what would happen to the flowers and the honey. Then I noticed something I hadn't before: A back-up crew of butterflies, wasps, and smaller bees were busy flitting from flower to flower, drinking nectar, spreading pollen, and keeping the whole thing going. And when I think of that — or the dance between our earth and moon — I think, Whoa, it's all connected, and it all works out.

Which makes me sense a perfect wisdom, just watching it unfold.

. . . .

"My religion consists of a humble admiration of the illimitable superior spirit who reveals himself in the slight details we are able to perceive with our frail and feeble mind."

— ALBERT EINSTEIN

. . .

"As the poet said, 'Only God can make a tree' — probably because it's so hard to figure out how to get the bark on."

— WOODY ALLEN

LOVE NATURE

I always loved nature — trees and such — but I grew up in an urban family that was scared of spiders and considered a good outing to be a trip to the diner. It wasn't until later that my love for nature bloomed.

There are two ways to love nature. The first is with all your senses. Earth and sun, wind and water — each has an energy we can connect with.

To feel my connection to the earth, I like to touch it with my hands, or walk barefoot, or lie down on the silky grass, breathe in its smell, and watch the clouds, the way I did when I was seven.

In summer months, I look for chances to swim in the ocean or bay, the warm sun on my face as I flow with the water. And on dark summer nights, I walk out naked on our balcony to feel the cool breeze against my skin.

A second way to love nature is to protect it. You pick one part you truly care about — the changing climate, our wildlife, the bees — and do what you can to save it. With that intention, our Bioregional Group read the booklet *50 Ways to Help the Planet* and began to practice the many ways. I started with No. 16, "Brush Without Running," which advised me to turn off the spigot while brushing my teeth. At first it seemed like no big deal. I mean, even if everyone did it, how much water would be saved? Then the book told me: "Daily savings in the U.S. alone could add up to 1.5 billion gallons."

So I still turn off the water when I brush my teeth. It reminds me that I care. And it's through small acts of caring that we learn to love.

STAY CLOSE TO NATURE

Staying close to nature is simple: Get outside and be there. Walk by the river, sit in the park, and watch and listen.

When I lived in Manhattan, I felt impelled now and then to leave the city and head for the country, where I could hear the birds, smell fresh air, and see the stars that city lights hide. We need time spent in nature just as surely as we need food and shelter. It soothes our soul, calms our mind, and can even heal our pain.

A lifetime ago, when my first marriage fell apart, I received this message in a fortune cookie: *There are three great healers: Time, Love, and Nature.* Being a strong believer in fortune cookies, I taped it to the fridge, and then I waited for it to prove true.

I remember days when, frozen with anxiety, I sat outside all morning to feel the sun's warmth. I remember nights when I cried to the moon and felt only the sky could hold my sorrow. I remember walks through the woods, breathing in the smell of pine trees, and feeling my spirit slowly lift.

Over time, with the love of friends and my children and the power of nature, I began to heal. The fortune cookie was right. And so was Frank:

> *Study nature,*
> *Love Nature,*
> *Stay close to nature.*
> *It will never fail you.*

Part Seven

SACRED SPACE.
SACRED TIME.

You want the whole world to be
your sacred space, and it is.
But we forget, so our sacred space
is a reminder.

THE MAGIC HOUR

Dawn and dusk, some believe, are the best times to pray. They do seem to have a holy aura. Especially dawn, when birds are singing their hearts out and the day smells fresh and clean. And dawn announces something else: the Magic Hour.

The Magic Hour earned its name from photographers, to describe this time when they love to shoot. It's the first and last half-hour of sunlight, starting just before the sun rises and just before it sets. Sometimes it lasts longer, sometimes it's shorter, and sometimes, on cloudy days, it doesn't happen at all. The truth is, you can't pin down magic. But what *is* certain is that when the sun is close to the horizon, it casts a soft golden light on everything you see, causing the Magic Hour to also be known as the Golden Hour.

The first time I saw it I was in college. It was a late afternoon in autumn, and I was walking across campus, kicking leaves with my friend Karen, who suddenly said, "Look!" I turned to look back at the Gothic towers of our dorm, and everything was suffused with a warm golden glow. The old stone buildings and clusters of fir trees looked clearer yet softer, like a picture in perfect focus but shot through gauze.

"Wow," I said. "Is this what the world's *really* like? Or is it just an illusion?"

Karen muttered something about how the subjective mind can never know objective reality. We were both
"phil" majors, and that's how we talked.

I don't remember what we decided, but I do know this:
The effect at its fullest only lasts a few minutes, yet it's always
worth seeking. For the magic hour is not only the best time
to pray or take photos; it's a time to step out, bask in the
light, and be a witness. On most days, what you'll see is this:
a world lit up and resplendent, its glory and magic revealed.
And all *you* have to do is be there.

ZEN VIEW

It was a long, hot day in a long, hot summer. I noticed without surprise that all the flowers in our garden had died, and the only color besides brown was the green of their drooping leaves. It was also the day that our friend Sarah was being operated on for brain cancer. And that morning, in some worrisome synchronicity, my mom found a lump on her breast, while I discovered a hard, suspect lump in my cheek.

My goal was to stay positive: to hold Sarah in the light, have faith in her healing, and believe that Mom and I would also be fine. I had come to the garden to feel uplifted, but it looked so dreary I only felt worse.

Perhaps some deep watering will help, I thought, this being a chore I enjoy. It instantly connects me to each plant and allows me to notice how they've changed. So I grabbed the hose and began. And as I started watering all those drab, flowerless plants, a curious thing happened. First, I spotted some wild daisies. Then I found tiny yellow asters, hiding behind some dusty leaves, while off to the side, the first pink blooms on the Rose of Sharon had just opened, so soft and lovely they made me sigh. Why, it's a lovely garden, I thought, but subtle. You have to move around to see it. You have to find the zen view.

I first heard about the zen view when John and I were building our house (a time of dreams and nightmares, as anyone crazy enough to do this knows). Someone lent us a tome entitled *A Pattern Language: Towns, Buildings, Construction,* written by a group of architects and urban planners. The authors had studied design and building in cultures throughout the world, searching for the underlying principles, the archetypes that work and endure. Then they distilled these into patterns to help others create the ideal town, city, or home.

In that crazy, intense time, John and I read the book avidly and talked in patterns, hoping our house would be harmonious, that it would truly be a home.

One of the patterns the authors encourage is the zen view, which is fleeting and restrained. Not for them those picture windows looking out at showy mountains that you stare at all day long. They prefer that you follow a path from your door and maybe enter a courtyard where through a narrow slit in a stone wall you catch a distant sighting of those same mountains. The zen view is something you glimpse in passing and that comes as a surprise — to wake you to the moment and a flash of hidden truth.

So today I enjoyed a zen view of our mid-summer garden. And when I walked along the driveway, I found another zen view in our meadow: a sleeping fawn half-hidden by tall grasses. My spirit lifted as I remembered the spaciousness of life.

Back in the house, though, my thoughts soon returned to Sarah in the hospital and Mom's lump and mine, and all my fears revived. I could feel them in my stomach, churning away.

Then something happened that made everything shift. The doorbell rang and it was Marianne, a fellow member of our Friends of Darfur group. She had come to pick up yard signs we'd recently made. I always liked Marianne. Her down-to-earth manner and dry humor helped our group stay real. On this hot day, I offered her a cool drink, and when she asked me how I was, I answered, "Scared," as my eyes began to tear.

"What's happening?" Marianne asked kindly, and I told her — about Sarah, Mom, and me. I didn't know her well, but maybe that's why I opened up. And when I stopped talking, she opened up too. Years ago, she said, she was in Quebec when her heart stopped. They rushed her to a hospital for emergency surgery. Then she went into a coma and they flew her to Los Angeles, not really believing that she would live. But all the time she was conscious she found herself saying a prayer from her childhood, the Hebrew prayer *Sh'ma:* "Hear O Israel, the Lord our God, the Lord is One!"

"It was so strange," Marianne said in her matter-of-fact way. "I was never religious before then." She looked at me and shrugged. "I don't know what made me say that prayer. But I know that's what saved me."

Now, I can't say my dark feelings never returned that day. Yet I knew a sense of grace would also return, indirectly and when least expected. Like the first blooms on the Rose of Sharon, or the sleeping fawn, or Marianne. It's the way our world works, the way it was made, with a zen view waiting to show us the light.

A SACRED SPACE

The first time I saw a "sacred space" in someone's home was in the 1970s. I was visiting my friend Mary in Cambridge and she said I could stay over — if I didn't mind sleeping on a mattress on the floor of her "meditation room."

"No problem," I said. For those were the days when I attended retreats at Zen monasteries, where the beds were so hard I was almost grateful when the bells woke us up to chant before dawn.

No bells at Mary's. Just a room that looked restful: soft white rug, the noted mattress, and some candles. The emptiness of the room was soothing. It invited me to empty my mind.

But having a sacred space in your home doesn't require a whole room; it can evolve in a simple space. A bookcase, window, or corner can easily become the site for creating altars or tableaux of meaningful objects and images, ones that resonate for you.

Larger spaces can become places to pray, meditate, or rest in, if they offer privacy and quiet at least some of the time. My sacred space is in an alcove off our bedroom. I often pass it without looking. But once I sit down on the prayer rug, light the candles, and begin to meditate or do yoga, I forget the larger room behind me and I'm back in my sacred space. I guess it's what I bring to it — my intention and practice — that makes it feel sacred. And by creating an inspiring environment, my intention and practice have deepened.

Some people may already have a sacred space in their home but not think of it that way. For my mother, it's her kitchen table, next to a wall of family photos. "When things are troubling me," Mom says, "I go there and sit. Then I have a cup of coffee and think things through, until I'm feeling better. I never thought of it as my sacred space, but I guess it is."

Other people find their sacred space outdoors: a bench with a view in their garden, or a hidden grove in a nearby park.

And some people, like our neighbor Brian Spielmann, have enough space to create a dedicated shrine room with Buddhist hangings — an uptown version of Mary's meditation room-cum-mattress. Brian goes there to meditate or make offerings, and he goes there every day.

"You want the whole world to be your sacred space," he says, "and it is. But we forget, so our sacred space is a reminder."

A SACRED HOME

John and I wanted our whole home to feel sacred, so
we nailed on our doorpost a *mezuzah:* an encased parchment scroll inscribed with prayers from the Torah. It's a
Jewish tradition to protect families and to remind us, as
we come and go, of the sacredness of world and home.
*("Sacred, schmacred!" my dad mutters in heaven. "If you're Jewish, you
hang a mezuzah. End of story!")* Right.

Another way we made our home feel sacred was
through its design. We built arches between rooms, because we liked how they looked and felt. I later learned
that in some eastern countries, walking under an arch is
considered a mystical passage. We also put in skylights,
which let in sunbeams and moonlight and connect us to
the natural world.

To feel more connected to the house itself, we walk
through it barefoot or wearing slippers, having made our
home shoe-free. It felt strange at first; but now I find
that just by removing my shoes at the door, I begin to feel
this space is special. It makes me feel special too. *("Good,"
my dad says. "But me, I'll wear shoes.")* Sure, Dad, whatever.

Then there's feng shui, an ancient Chinese practice.
It's a way to bring good energy into your home and life —
through proper placement of objects and colors and the
harmonious use of water and wind. For us, it was a last
resort. Because of the ghost.

It all started with the contractor, who said he'd help build us the house of our dreams. He seemed perfectly skilled and honest, but he was neither. Every day something broke or made problems. And when his budget ran out, he did too — but not before telling me the house was haunted and blaming that for all that went wrong.

Now, I never really believed in ghosts, but his words stayed with me, like a curse. And once we moved in, the energy of the house did seem, well, askew. Which is why we asked Sawada, a Buddhist monk we knew, for help.

Buddhists believe in a ghost realm and have ceremonies for blessing homes. Sawada came in his saffron robes, sat on the floor with John and me, and chanted prayers in Sanskrit. When he was done, I asked if the ghosts were gone. "No," he said, "but don't worry. I made them Buddhists!"

Okay, I admit it: Buddhist ghosts sounded friendlier. Still, I wanted them out.

So I read three books on feng shui and following their guidance, we totally cleaned and de-cluttered our house and blessed it — with the help of Jeanne V., our friend and neighborhood shaman. Jeanne led us from room to room while banging her drum and saying "Begone!" to scare off ghosts and other bad sorts. "House blessings," Jeanne explained, "let you clean your house on an energetic level." Then she lit some sage, waved it in every corner, and said, "Just like temple-keepers, we need to keep purifying the space where we live."

(While all this clearing and cleansing was going on, I could hear my dad chuckling above, "Fung shway, Oy Vey! I was hocking her to clean her room since she was ten!")

Another neighbor who helped harmonize our home — and kick out the ghosts — was Laurelyn, a feng shui consultant. Once you create sacred space, she said, the walls of your home become more permeable, so nature and magic can start coming in. We followed most of her advice, and our house really did feel lighter, more flowing, ghost-free.

But the best thing she taught us was this: When you open your house to others with love, that's when your home becomes sacred and blessed.

("You got it!" says Dad. "Now you're cooking with gas!")

ONE HOLY DAY

I met John for dinner at Shanghai Gourmet. Like most restaurants that call themselves "gourmet," it's anything but. The food is fair and a little bland; you pick up your order when they call your name; and the seats in the booths are patched up with tape.

It wasn't until we sat down to eat that I remembered it was Sabbath. For many years now, we'd been lighting candles and blessing the wine and bread each Friday. It makes that time special and lends an aura of peace.

"It's Sabbath!" I said, feeling sad we'd forgotten.

"No worries," John replied. And my good Church-of-England husband pulled out from his jacket pocket some wrapped-up bread, a votive candle, and a tiny wine cup half-filled with Manishevitz. We lit the candle and the blessings began.

Friday nights, when I was young, meant dinner at Nana's. The table was set with a white lace cloth; a dish of black olives sat between the Sabbath candles; and there was ginger ale with ice in tall crystal glasses — the sharp kind of ginger ale that fizzed into your nose. Everything was always the same; everything felt like a ritual. Sometimes we'd get there early and find Nana scrubbing the house. She did it so intently, I thought this was another ritual. Just one more part of keeping Sabbath. I still think so. And when I clean our house well, especially on Fridays, it seems to take on a glow, and I do too.

You don't have to be Jewish to keep Sabbath, and it can be any day you choose: one day each week, sundown to sundown, that's set apart by the way you spend it.

For a few years, I honored Sabbath by fasting, which almost always makes me high. Then I considered making Saturday a day of silence; but alas, I'm a talker, and talkers talk. What I did stop doing, though, is work. And that gives me the gift of time: to sit and do nothing, to call people I've been meaning to call, or to immerse myself in nature.

Judaism considers Sabbath the most important holiday of all. It's a time to give thanks for the creation of the world, and a day to celebrate with joy, rest, and holiness. For me, the holiest part is at sundown, when we light the candles and say the blessings.

When my kids were young, we kept a simple Sabbath: The table held two candles, which I lit and blessed. Then Tony blessed the wine, Elise blessed the hallah, and I blessed the children. With the three of us standing, I placed my hands lightly on their little heads — on Elise's bouncy curls and Tony's silky straight hair — and recited the prayer in Hebrew and English: "May God bless you and keep you. May God cause his countenance to shine upon you, and be gracious unto you, and grant you peace." Something about that blessing felt so good I'd almost cry.

Now, with John, I end by saying this: "May the light from these candles come into our hearts and into the world."

That's what I said at Shanghai Gourmet, just before we ate our chow mein.

Part Eight

SOUL FOOD

I always felt that food was sacred.
At first, I thought it was a Jewish thing.
Not only because we love to eat, but because
we celebrate our holy days around the table,
with special foods for each.

MRS. ZIMNOSKI
AND HER VEGETABLES

When I lived in Manhattan, I spent time each summer at
a farm in eastern Long Island. The farm was a refuge for
me, a balance to my life in the city. It was a place to dream
in ... with cornfields, wild flowers, and a road you could
walk on forever. And each year, before I'd leave, I'd visit
Mrs. Zimnoski, an older woman who lived one farm away.

Sometimes I believed the visits were for her. She
must be lonely, I told myself. Twenty years a widow. But
no matter why I went, I always left feeling better, carrying
home her just-picked tomatoes.

Each visit was much like the other. I'd walk past
her vegetable garden, ring her kitchen door, and peer
through the window to see her approaching. Short and
buxom, she'd be wearing a large flowered housedress and
holding a broom or wooden spoon since she was always
busy doing something — cooking, tending her garden,
or cleaning the house. Soft grey curls framed her sun-
wrinkled face, and bifocals gave her round eyes a look of
constant surprise.

"Whoooo?" she'd call out, her voice rising in
question. Then, opening the door, she'd exclaim,
"What! Missus!" and we'd collapse into hugs with her
chirping like a bird.

Born in Poland, but living here since she was ten, she still spoke with a heavy accent and mixed her "he's" and "she's" with confusing abandon. It was like being at the opera: I'd get the drift of her stories, but they were clouded in mystery, never fully known.

When I'd take Tony and Elise along to see her, she'd always find some raisin cookies still warm from the oven, which she'd serve with tall glasses of tart cherry juice. "I tell you story," she'd say to them, "of when I been little goil." Then she'd furrow her brow and squint her eyes before recounting pieces of her childhood: growing up on a dairy farm in Poland, meeting Russians and gypsies, witnessing a war. And although my children understood her even less than I did, her excitement and laugher soon had them laughing too.

Sometimes I'd take my friends there to meet her, and she'd be so pleased to have all this "young" company that she'd bring out and pour for them her dandelion wine. "Is good?" she'd ask eagerly, as they savored its honey-lemon taste. "Mmmm," they'd respond and ask how it's made.

It was a story I never tired of hearing: Mrs. Zimnoski, every spring, bending her small, stout body and picking with fingers gnarled from arthritis hundreds of dandelions from the fields nearby. Then, carrying them home in buckets to her kitchen, where she'd boil and ferment them to create her old-time brew. It was an image I cherished, for it let me know that no matter how bad the world might seem, something good and right was enduring — and nearby.

Although I'd known her for more than a decade, we never spoke of inner things; we didn't even use first names. It took years of visits to learn that she was christened Marcella, but since she insisted on calling me "Missus," I always called her Mrs. Zimnoski. Only once did she ask me anything personal:

"The children's father, he's good to them?"

Yes.

"He never hit you?'

No.

"He drink?"

No.

"So why you get divorced?"

If only life were that simple, I thought, and wondered if it could be and if, for her, it was. But all I knew for sure that was simple was the way she lived, the same hard work with which she structured her days, the focus on what is and what has to be done, with no time to worry about what could or should have been.

I guess she was my teacher, someone I was meant to meet. There was one summer, though, when I almost didn't see her. I was too busy searching for answers. Not simple answers, but things like meaning, certainty, and strength. I walked miles on that country road, trying only to silence the chatter in my mind. The farm's magic hadn't worked. And I hadn't seen Mrs. Zimnoski.

I was feeling too anxious for idle chatter, too self-involved for cookies and juice. Still, I finally decided to visit since I didn't know how soon I'd be back. So I stopped by, ate some of her fresh sauerkraut, and listened to her talk.

"Look!" she commanded and showed me a cauliflower just picked from her garden. "Look how beautiful!" she said. It did look beautiful, jewel-like, with its creamy white florets and pale green leaves, the brown soil still clinging to its roots.

She went on to tell me the four vegetables Farmer Dabrowski said could keep you from getting cancer. "Cabbage, cauliflower, Brussel sprouts ... what else he tell me? I not remember what she say."

I was only half-listening, too distracted to respond.

"Broccoli? ... Onions?" she mused, half talking to herself, half talking to me.

"Beets?" I said, somewhat soothed by this conversation.

"Beets," I repeated, looking out the kitchen window to potato fields beyond.

"Cabbage," Mrs. Zimnoski murmured, counting the litany on her fingers.

I realized we were talking vegetables, yet not really talking at all. It was as if we had entered together some country meditation where the mantra was "cabbage, cauliflower, Brussel sprouts, and beets." And for a few minutes, the voices in my mind were stilled, as I rested in the goodness and clarity of vegetables.

Then, time to go. Hugs and chirping until I left: feeling better, as always, and carrying home her ripest tomatoes.

SACRED SOUND BITES

Food is alive. I forget that sometimes, until I reach up and pick an apple from our tree.

A Jewish thing.
I always felt that food was sacred. At first, I thought it was a Jewish thing. Not only because we loved to eat (and had a Jewish mother urging us on), but also because we celebrate our holy days around the table, with special foods for each.

On Sabbath, we bless the wine and hallah and give thanks to the Lord, "who creates the fruit of the vine" and "brings forth bread from the earth." On Rosh Hashanah, the Jewish New Year, we eat apples dipped in honey to bless the year with sweetness. And on Passover, we eat matzah, unleavened bread, to remember our ancestors who were slaves fleeing Egypt and had no time to let the bread rise. We eat the matzah with bitter herbs and bless them both.

But, I soon learned, this is not just a Jewish thing; it's universal. All religions and indigenous cultures agree: Food is sacred, the source of life. It's something to give thanks for every day.

"One eats in holiness and the table becomes an altar"

— MARTIN BUBER

There is a Zen monastery in upstate New York that's housed in an old mansion along the Hudson River. I went there with a group for a weekend retreat, and after a long day of chanting and meditation, we gathered together at a long table for dinner. But before we were served, the Zen master said a prayer — a *long* prayer — thanking the earth, the sun, the air, and the rain, the farmers, the cook, and everyone else who helped grow or prepare our food and bring it to the table. Then he asked us to be silent, eat slowly, and appreciate each taste. The meal was spare, yet it felt like a feast.

The other meals I've eaten in holiness, albeit a rowdier version, were at Helen and Allan's home on a pine-treed mountainside in Jamestown, Colorado. John and I would sit with them and their children around a wooden table near the fire, and before we'd eat, we'd all hold hands. Sometimes it was enough to just do that and feel the energy pass between us. But it got even better when they'd start singing with gusto a full-bodied rendition of grace:

> *Thank you for the world so sweet,*
> *Thank you for the food we eat,*
> *Thank you for the birds that sing,*
> *Thank you, God, for everything!*

This was followed by a loud series of "Yums" in raucous harmony.

John and I now say this prayer almost nightly. And when we sing it with our young grandsons Eli and Isaac, they get so excited to be singing, blessing, and holding hands at dinner that they ask us to sing it "again!" and "again!"

All food is sacred. But some foods seem more sacred than others.

Homemade soup and home-baked bread (making it, smelling it, eating it!).

Southern fried chicken and collard greens (Black soul food).

Tea and scones with clotted cream and jam (English soul food).

Corn-on-the-cob with salt and butter (sacred enough that the Indians do a Corn Dance).

Refried beans, rice, and salsa (Mexican soul food).

Warm milk with honey (which they'd serve us each night at the yoga ashram before we'd chant and go to bed).

Chocolate (which the Huichol Indians believe is a gift from paradise and leave as an offering at places of prayer).

Bagels and lox with cream cheese and olives (Jewish soul food).

And, best of all, food fresh from the garden.

From the garden.

Annie and Ellie created a huge vegetable garden. It became a community project, with friends and neighbors pitching in: plowing, weeding, and sowing. It was a beautiful garden, with plantings in spirals and Buddhist flags hanging from the fence.

"Take anything you want," Annie said, when she

proudly led me through it. I took three heads of lettuce
and some baby chard.

Our own garden was more modest. Still, it took
work: John digging, me weeding, and both watering each
day. But the reward for our work came in August when
I'd be making a soup or salad and run outside to pick
cherry tomatoes and leaves of sweet basil to toss in at the
end — fresh from the earth, straight to the table.

There's something special about eating foods you plant
and tend. Annie says it's because you have a relationship
with it from all that work you did to help it grow.

Light a candle.

Before I make dinner, I sometimes light a candle and maybe
say a prayer to bless the meal. I especially like to do this when
company is coming and I'm cursing the clock and wondering why I ever thought I could make fish, rice, and spinach
all be done at the same time. Calm down, the candlelight
says. And more often than not, I do.

Tortillas.

When we visit Mexico, one of my favorite jaunts is walking
to the village *tortilleria* in the early morning when the roost-
ers are still crowing and stray dogs are barking. I enter the
shop, smell the freshly baked tortillas, and buy a dozen for
ten pesos. Lined up behind me are old women and young
girls who buy a much larger stack of soft corn tortillas to
fill with eggs and chilies, or rice and beans, or maybe fresh
fish for dinner.

My tortillas are wrapped in brown paper to keep
them warm. I feel their heat as I carry them back to our
casita. The butter melts on them at breakfast.

Cooking together.

Sure, there was sex, drugs, and rock 'n' roll. But what really kept the hippy communes going was the outright fun of cooking together — and making something finer than you'd ever make alone.

The year I met John, we spent our first New Year's Eve at a small cottage in Vermont. Outside, there was nothing but piles of snow, and you couldn't walk out without freezing your nose. Inside, we cooked an English feast: parsnips, jacket potatoes, Brussel sprouts, and carrots — preceded by Cheshire cheese and crusty bread and toasted with champagne. It was the first time we cooked together, and it deepened our bond.

The body-mind connection.

It's well known that our mind affects our body (with stress causing disease, and placebos working if we believe in them). But the opposite is also true: Our body and what we put into it can affect our mind and mood.

When I eat light, I feel light, physically and spiritually. I first became aware of this when I attended retreats where the meals were modest and vegetarian — brown rice with lentils, that sort of fare.

But I also love hot fudge sundaes, Elise's butter-cream cakes, and the high I get from two margaritas. What can I say? I guess "moderation." "Everything's fine in moderation," said Aristotle. Or maybe it was my mother.

THE HUMBLE OATMEAL

In the 1980s, I was a social worker in Harlem, directing a program that helped kids stay in school. At that time, nearly seventy percent of minority children dropped out, and what I learned made me understand why. They were scared of rats in their bedrooms and junkies on the street; their teachers were happy when they didn't show up; and almost every child I worked with had seen someone get killed — their father or brother or friend.

One autumn day I looked out the barred windows of one of the schools and saw a brilliant blue sky. "Look how beautiful it is," I said to Lakisha, a nine-year-old I felt drawn to and was teaching to read during lunch. She answered dully, "It's ugly here, Miss." And suddenly, through her eyes, I saw it all in stark relief: the boarded-up tenements, the wandering homeless, the treeless streets littered with garbage.

That's when I knew I had to do more, something more radical than my everyday job. I wanted to get to the bottom of things: to clean up drugs and crime; to create great schools so all kids have a chance; to end poverty, racism, and injustice. Simply put, I wanted to save the world. But how?

It was around that time that I saw a flyer for a workshop in Massachusetts. It was titled "Follow Your Calling." So I signed on and landed up in a rural farmhouse, where there were only a few participants besides myself. Ironically, though, one of the few was a man who also saw his "calling" as saving the world. I sensed a subtle competition, and we didn't really click — which was unfortunate, since teaming up might have made the job a lot easier.

But as it turned out, the workshop leader, Sally, thought my goal was a bit sweeping and suggested I think smaller. Maybe help save one little piece of the world. And maybe start with me.

"One way to find your calling," Sally announced, "is to know what makes you happy." Then she asked us all to make a list of whatever makes us happy and take it from there.

Makes me happy ....

I jotted down the first thoughts that came to mind:

Nature

Love

Helping Others

Oatmeal

Oatmeal? Why oatmeal? Who knows. Perhaps it was childhood memories: my mother making oatmeal on a cold winter day. The comfort of eating it with toast and jam. And I'm talking real, not instant, oatmeal, the kind you have to cook and watch and stir. A hippie slogan around that time was "You are what you eat." Well, I wanted to be oatmeal: simple, healthy, and close to the earth. And when I *eat* oatmeal, that's kind of how I feel.

Getting back to my list, I looked at "helping others" and remembered all the children in Harlem I had come here to save but didn't know how. Then I remembered teaching Lakisha to read, how excited she was with each new word, and how good it felt to have something real I could offer.

With that in mind I wrote down "teaching," right below "oatmeal." I envisioned having my own kids in my own classroom, where I would give them love and support and teach them to read — things that just might change their lives.

So I left the workshop knowing this: I would make and eat oatmeal a few times a week and go back to school to become a teacher.

It wasn't long after then that I met John, an Englishman passing through New York. This was fortuitous. Not only was John changing his life course at the same time I was, and not only did he smile and say gently, "Well, I never thought of saving the world, though I do try to make it a little better," but, like most Brits, he loved oatmeal (which they call porridge), even for dinner. "It's an ancient grain," he said. "I think of monks in monasteries eating bowls of gruel."

One year later, John moved in with me, and one night a week we ate oatmeal. I stood and stirred it, just like my mom, and served it with toast and jam. It was a meal so humble it almost felt sacred.

Then, in the mornings, I took the crosstown bus to teach my young students. And that felt sacred too.

Part Nine

RITUALS AND CELEBRATIONS: Birth to Death and In-Between

Rituals are like ladders: They can take you to a higher place.

JOIN THE FAMILY

One year, after family plans fell through, John and I were destined to be home alone for Christmas. We were feeling quite dreary ... until we decided to go to Taos, the most magical place we know. We'd never been there in winter, but had heard about a Christmas Eve procession at the Taos Pueblo, the ancient village and longtime home of the Taos tribe. Now sometimes when we've visited reservations, I've left in sadness, feeling the sorrow of the people, their history, their land. But when we've attended their festivals — the Corn Dance, the Deer Dance — I've seen pride, spirit, and the power of tradition.

It's a long drive to Taos from Boulder, about five hours. We played tapes of Robert Mirabal most of the way. He's a flutist and singer who grew up in the Pueblo, and his songs blend native music with a sound called tribal rock. As we crossed the border leaving Colorado, the drumming on the tape grew mysteriously louder: Welcome to New Mexico, "Land of Enchantment."

On Christmas Eve, we parked at the edge of the reservation and followed hundreds of people — Spanish, Native, and Anglo — on a dirt road to the village. It was a moonless, wintry night, and most folks were walking briskly to stay warm. When we reached the open space in front of the chapel, next to 1,000-year-old dwellings made from mud and straw, we fell into clusters and a circle of sorts, and a buzz of excitement began to grow.

Church bells rang, and as if on cue, huge bonfires were lit, one by one, filling the black sky with golden flames and the sweet smell of burning pine. In the fires' glow I saw families and elders, all chatting, laughing, and smiling hellos. And there, right across from me, was Robert Mirabal! He looked just like the picture on the front of his tape — long black hair, leather boots — and he held a young child wrapped warmly in his arms. Then the fire shot up around us, blowing soot in my face, and I moved aside but stayed close enough to still feel its heat. I had never seen so many fires, nor any this high. It was almost frightening, yet exciting. It felt timeless and primal.

Just as the excitement was reaching its peak, from the courtyard of the church, the procession began: A painted wooden statue of the Virgin Mary, dressed in bridal white, was carried on a dais for all to see. Around and around the church folk carried her, slowly and reverently, while men behind them beat hand drums and chanted native chants. Next came the tribal dancers in headdresses and masks. Illuminated by the blazing fires, they stamped their feet to the droning rhythm played by musicians who followed. Lastly, I think, the carolers appeared, singing in Spanish and their native tongue of Tiwa.

There is no electricity within the village walls, but the flames from the fires leapt high in the darkness, as we huddled together, like a family, in the cold.

"It's about the sun returning," I heard someone say. "It gives us light for the new year," said another. It's Christmas, it's native, it's solstice, it's magic.

Looking back, it all feels like something I dreamed. But it happens every Christmas, and one year we were there.

HELLO TO DAD, NANA, UNCLE BOB, AND...

Every morning, after greeting the sun, I give a big hello to my ancestors as I look up at the southeastern sky. Why there? I'm not sure, but that's where I picture them hanging out. Some days my thoughts go just to my dad; some days to Rebecca, the grandmother I never knew but was named after; and sometimes I think of them all and say hello to each. There are a few I like a lot better now than I did when they were alive. That's the thing about death: You start to miss everyone after they're gone.

On some mornings, I thank my departed family for what they gave me — a memory, talent, or trait — and that alone recharges my love. When I'm feeling lost, I ask for their help, for courage, faith, or my dad's sense of humor. I also ask them to guide my children and, just as often, bless friends who are sick. I guess they're my own band of angels, ones I have real ties to.

These morning "hellos" are a way to honor my ancestors, to remember them and feel their presence in my life. At the same time, I gain a sense of connection to the vast, unseen realm they're now in, which somehow lessens my fear of death. And maybe, just maybe, when I die, they'll be there to greet me in the southeast corner of heaven. What can I say? I like Hollywood endings. What I'm hoping for is that God does too.

MEDITATIONS ON MEDITATION

I often think about meditating when I'm meditating. Like, Wow, this is cool, I'm really meditating! Of course, that instantly ruins it. Well, here are some thoughts about meditating, which I might have had while meditating.

It's nice to light a candle and ring a chime when I begin. It helps me enter a sacred space.

Dr. Michael Beckwith, the Reverend of Agape Church, suggests saying this when you start: "I'm here to wake up." And return to that thought when your thoughts go astray.

Meditation is not just this ancient ritual or hippie-guru kind of thing. It's also prosaic and down-to-earth. I mean, you're just sitting there, you know? And it's practical, like a good housecleaning, a cleansing of the mind.

I'm always reading books about meditation, and they always tell me the same thing: *Meditate! It's the path to peace — not to mention Nirvana and a sense of the divine.* Yes, yes, I nod. I'll do it! But then, instead of doing it, I read more books about it. So for thirty years, I've been a student of meditation: sometimes sitting daily, sometimes once a week ... but always up for another book.

Yet despite this predilection, a certain peace has managed to creep into my life. There are even moments of feeling, just as the books promise, the openness and spaciousness that some call God.

We sit on the ground with humbleness. But we sit up straight with dignity, since our body is the temple of our soul.

I used to hold off meditating until I was in a meditating mood: calm, serene, a little saintly. Well, some weeks I'd be waiting a long time. So I started taking my angry, worried, fearful self to the pillow. Not easy — some Nirvana! Still, the more I learn to just sit with my feelings, the more compassion I gain for myself, and the more compassion I feel for others. See? It all works out.

I once read that prayer is you talking to God and meditation is hearing God's answer. For me, both feel as if I'm phoning up the Source, making a connection — *Hello, God, are you there?* — and then, if *I'm* there, resting in God's grace.

Breathe in, breathe out; keep watching your breath. That's the way I first learned to meditate. It's called the breath-awareness meditation, which was part of the Buddha's teachings. Breathe in, breathe out, feel your breath where it enters and leaves your nose. Then, as your mind fills with thoughts and plans, or memories and worries, gently place your focus back on your breath.

So I sit, breathe in, and watch my breath, and my thoughts appear like clouds in the sky. What helps is to note them and let them pass through. "Thinking," I say to myself. "Pain, " I notice. "Planning." And then, as always, back to watching my breath.

Mary taught me the California quickie. In her studio in the woods of Topanga Canyon, we sat down together, she set the timer for five minutes, and then, in a far-off space and place, I rested briefly in a peace that felt timeless.

There are many versions of a loving-kindness meditation, which is a way of blessing the world. My version starts by breathing in love to myself. I imagine a golden light coming in with my breath and filling me from head to toe. When I breathe out, I picture that love and light going to others, surrounding them like an aura. I might start with my kids or mom or anyone I know who is suffering or in need. But whomever I start with, I ultimately imagine the light going farther — to troubled areas, our president, our planet. What surprises me is how sending love out feels even better than breathing love in.

Gay Lynn and I used to meditate together, the good old watch-your-breath way. Then Gay Lynn returned to Catholicism and found a way to meditate that touched her soul. It goes like this: Think of a word that signifies what you want to feel, such as love or peace or God, and keep returning to that thought when your mind drifts away.

I think of Divine Presence; and sometimes, as soon as I think it, a calm falls over me and I feel at peace.

So there I am, sitting in meditation and wondering yet again, *What* am I here for? *What* should I do? Oh yeah, watch my breath. But that's so boring, so nothing, so totally blah. Then I feel this great relief as I realize there is nothing — *nothing* — I have to do for these ten or twenty minutes: no thinking, no planning, no working in any way. I can just be bored or still and watch my breath. I surrender. *Ahhh.*

It's nice to ring a bell or a chime at the end. It gives a sense of closure, and the ritual's complete.

HEART LIKE A CRYSTAL

I went to see a shaman. Brant Secunda. He was down-home, funny, and grew up in New Jersey — my kind of shaman. So I signed up for his workshop: three days of teachings he learned from the Huichol Indians, a Mexican tribe that rescued him in the Sierra Madre Mountains. The young Brant had been searching for a spiritual teacher, but when he reached the jungles near Ixtlan, he became lost and sun-dazed and passed out. At the same time, the revered shaman Don José Matsuwa had a dream in which he saw Brant coming, and he sent his clansmen to save him.

Brant stayed in their village for eighteen years, living with this isolated tribe that followed age-old traditions. And Don José adopted Brant as his grandson and taught him all he knew through an arduous twelve-year apprenticeship.

"He put me in a cave without water for five days," Brant said. "He told me, 'If you die, the apprenticeship is over!'" Then, when Don José died at 110 (attributing his longevity to "not too much sex, only once a day"), he left Brant in his place to spread the Huichol wisdom.

In the workshop, Brant explained that shamanism is not just a form of healing, but a way of life. He taught us how to strengthen our connection with nature, to honor and heal Mother Earth.

We also learned a Huichol practice to heal our inner wounds. Negative emotions leave holes inside you, Brant said, but you can fill and cleanse those holes by sitting and facing the fire, sun, or a candle, and breathing in its light. "If you're fearful, imagine opening your throat and letting in the light. If you're angry, let the light into your stomach. If you're jealous, let it into your heart."

With plain talk and a modest manner, Brant spoke of amazing rituals and miracles he had seen. But what struck me most was the familiar, the common ground beneath. For under all their rituals and miracles, the Huichols were, like most people I know, simply looking for ways to deal with their emotions, connect with spirit, and become better people — which was why, Brant revealed, they use crystals.

That said, he opened a leather pouch, poured two dozen crystals onto a small Mexican rug, and asked each of us to choose one for our meditations.

Some of the crystals were so translucent you could see right through them. Others had a frosted appearance or mini-crystals within. I chose one of the latter, thinking its flaws made it more beautiful and would evoke a deeper meditation. Pleased with my pick, I felt a little sorry for those folks who had chosen ones that were boringly clear.

Then Brent said to make sure you liked your crystal; there was still time to change, and you wanted one that was as pure and transparent as possible since it would be a model for your heart. Aargh! I blew it. Humbled, I stepped forward and traded mine in for the clearest one left.

"Learn to harvest the light, brighten your spirit, and become crystal clear," Brant said, holding up a crystal as a purifying tool.

Till then, I had considered crystals New-Agey and was unaware of their long tradition. But reading a pamphlet that Brant passed out, I learned that the Huichol Indians have been using the crystal since ancient times "as a model for how our hearts should be. They strive to keep the crystal of their heart clear and vibrant so that light can shine through them ... and into the world."

When the workshop ended, I returned home and put the crystal on my altar. Now and then, I hold it up to remember: clear heart, open heart; one that sees my anger, envy, and fears ... and heals them by letting in light.

"Nobody's perfect," Brant told us, "but we try to make ourselves better."

And so, each day, I aim to do my best, to think of others and be kind. Sounds easy, right? Not. What helps is knowing what I strive for: a heart like a crystal. It also helps knowing that far off in the Sierra Madres, there's a tribe of Huichol Indians, and they're striving for that too.

. . . .

Create in me a pure heart O God.

— PSALMS 51:10

SISTER JUDY'S CALIFORNIA
MEDITATION RECIPE

My sister Judy was a wheelin'-dealin' lawyer-screenwriter in Hollywood. Then she found God (or vice versa), and it changed her life. She moved to Playa del Rey, became a spiritual counselor, and now starts each day with meditation on the beach.

She begins by reading some inspirational writings. Then she closes her eyes or looks out at the ocean and puts all her attention on feeling God's love, returning that love, and feeling gratitude for that love. "Breathe in the presence of God," she says, "and breathe out love and peace and healing."

"What if you don't *feel* God's love?" a friend asked when I told her. I answered the way I thought Judy would: Just feel God's love in whatever form it comes to you, which could be your child, mate, friends, or pet; or the sky or mountains; or the joy you know in being alive.

"Imagination is a powerful tool," Judy says. "I might envision golden dust falling on someone I'm thinking of in healing prayer."

When her morning meditation is over, she spends the rest of her day "seeing the magic in everything and everywhere I go." But she always holds a stone to keep herself grounded.

Our mother likes to keep her grounded too. She was a tad concerned with Judy's transformation and wondered why she couldn't just be a wheelin'-dealin' lawyer-screenwriter who meditated. In truth, we were all a bit concerned, especially at first, when Judy just didn't seem like Judy.

But now, it's hard not to be touched by her sincere love of God and the radiance it brings her. And Judy's meditation sounds radiant too: buoyant and full of light, like California or the ocean.

When I first heard it, I remembered being in a Hindu temple at dusk. There was incense burning, and a smiling Swami sat at the front, leading us in *kirtan*, responsive chanting of the names of God. Six white-robed musicians were playing drums, bells, and harmonium, creating haunting melodies as we sang in Sanskrit, *"Hari Krishna, Hari Rama, Hari, Hari, Rama, Rama."*

It's part of a worship called Bhakti Yoga — the path of devotion, the path of the Heart — that's said to be the quickest way to reach the divine.

"Surrender," the Swami urged us, "to something far greater ...."

Then the music got faster and faster as we chanted louder and louder, and soon nearly everyone was standing and swaying, arms up, palms open, as we sang and danced with a love or bliss that spread and soared throughout the room.

When sister Judy meditates, she's in that temple dancing.

GREETING THE SEASONS

One thing I like about the seasons is how they always show up on time. Just as I'm turning the calendar to September 21, sure enough, the air gets crisper, a slight frost is seen, and I can smell the ripe apples that now lie on the ground. It's that way with each season, right on time, proving yes, the world is turning, and as surely as winter is here, spring is coming, no worries.

Living in Boulder, home of New Age trends, I've become more aware of the solstice, the equinox, and ways to celebrate each. But there's nothing New Age about these markers of the seasons. As celestial events they've been celebrated for thousands of years. And, uniquely, they offer us this: a day on which to welcome each season and feel more in sync with the earth and all life.

It could be enough just to keep track of these dates, to write down and know when each season begins. On those days, I decorate our home with gourds, or pinecones, or branches of yellow forsythia. And sometimes I do something special, in groups or with John, to celebrate the change and what the new season means.

The summer solstice comes on June 21 and is the first day of summer. It's the longest, most light-filled day of the year.

On June 21, 2007, the early sunlight woke us by 6, and that's when John suggested that we walk to the lake. I was feeling a little wistful, not as excited about Boulder, nature, or the solstice as I was when we first moved here. That was long ago, though, so I guess it could be expected. You get used to things, even glorious things, like mountains and starlight and the one you love. But then, on another day, all the glory comes back.

Besides, even feeling wistful, it was nice to take this walk. We saw redwing blackbirds, heard the meadowlark sing, and spotted our first dragonfly of the season. When we reached the lake's small sandy shore, we looked out at the ducks, saw jumping fish in the water, and considered what ritual to do.

Sometimes the best ritual is whatever comes to mind. On this day, we decided to simply give thanks, thanks for the gifts of summer.

"Thank you for the sunshine," I started.

"And the long days," John said, "and warmth."

"Thank you for the return of the dragonfly."

"For corn and peaches."

"And swimming in warm water."

"Thank you for summer."

Low-key, but nice.

The next day, in our local paper, there was a picture of Aymara Indians near La Paz, Bolivia. They were holding up their hands to catch the first rays of dawn as they celebrated the Southern Hemisphere's *winter* solstice, the beginning of the Aymara New Year. And later, on the radio, we heard that hundreds of New Yorkers had gathered to do sun salutations all day long — on a traffic island in the middle of Times Square.

Each solstice and equinox is a cosmic dance. I was happy now that we had joined in.

. . . .

"Don José always used to say, 'We make it rain with our ceremonies.' Which impressed me a lot. And then he said, 'But I'm not stupid. Before I make it rain, I wait for the rainy season.' So, you know, you work in harmony with the seasons."

— BRANT SECUNDA,
Huichol shaman

LOOKING FOR LIGHT

In the 1960s, a diverse group of people set out on a journey. We had no idea where we were going. In fact, we were searching for a path, a higher path to follow.

Like most of my fellow pilgrims, I had long abandoned organized religion, but was left with a yearning for something more, a way to touch life more deeply. So there we were, a few million of us, meditating, learning yoga, and looking for light in more easterly places — where ecstatic chants and silent retreats seemed to promise enlightenment and mystical bliss.

With that promise in mind, I attended a mega-event in New York City starring someone billed as The Sufi Master of the West. Tall and white-bearded, he was a soft-spoken man. But what got me was the warm-up act by a Hasidic rabbi. (A rabbi? I thought. How did *he* sneak in?) His name was Zalman Schachter-Shalomi.

He laughed and wagged his finger like a Jewish St. Nick. He joked. He schmoozed. And then he went for the kill. I don't recall his exact words, but the gist went like this:

You're looking for God? You've lost your way? Forget the bells and whistles. Just get down and pray!

Now, he wasn't talking church prayer or prayers you recite by rote or from a book. No, he meant prayers from the heart, fresh and alive with our own words and feelings.

Pray from your soul, he said, from your kishkes, *your guts. Prayer, he said, is simply talking to God.*

What? Share my deepest hopes and fears? Find *my* words and *my* God? This was something I had never heard before. Yet hearing it felt familiar, like coming home.

I didn't know then that he was passing on (in his uniquely Zalman way) the teachings of the Hasidic founders, who taught their students to sit alone, indoors or out, and simply open their hearts to God.

Whatever comes to mind, say it. You don't even have to believe — and you can say that too.

"Prayer," Reb Zalman said, "is simply talking to God."

So that's what I started to do. Simple, but not easy. I mean, to say what I really want to say (and not feel self-conscious or worry if God will like me), to be that honest and real (instead of showing God how *good* I am), well, it's a challenge. Still, there is the freedom of authenticity: Anything goes.

The way I begin is always changing. I might start with Great Spirit, or Dear Lord, or Blessed Mother ... or all three. I might even say "Divine Friend" and remember what my Sufi teacher said: "Just imagine you're talking to a special friend or your higher spirit."

Sometimes I pray for others; sometimes for the world; and sometimes for myself. I often pray for answers, and just as often to give thanks. Some days my prayers are affirmations: "I'm living with calmness and kindness." And some nights my prayer is a song, an Episcopal hymn I first heard in the musical *Godspell*:

> *"To see thee more clearly*
> *Love thee more dearly*

Follow thee more nearly
Day by Day."

The funny thing is, when I need it the most, I often forget to pray. That's what makes dark nights of the soul so dark: I lose my connection to spirit or anything else. At some point, though, just before touching bottom, I remember to pray: for strength, for peace, for help. Truth is, it doesn't matter what I pray for; it's prayer itself that helps bring me back.

I once took a workshop in which they asked, "What do you want more than anything else?" I answered "faith," because I knew that with faith, anything could seem bearable and most things were possible. I still feel that way; and sometimes my faith is strong, while other times it's lacking. But when my faith is at its weakest, I recall what Swami Vishwananda said: No one's faith is strong just like that. You have to build it, day by day.

Right. But how do you build faith? That's when I remember again to pray: Pray for faith.

My prayers can also be mundane and specific. For a long time, I obsessed over a major decision: to leave our happy life in Boulder and move back East — closer to kids, grandkids, and Mom — or stay out West, missing meaningful family moments and perhaps dying alone (in a dark room on a grey, wintry day). Now I have trouble even choosing a new mattress (even though John and I have talked about it for ten years and the coils of our old one stick into my back), so how could I ever decide anything as huge as a move? I told my friend Mary this, and she said, "You're right. This is too big to figure out. Let it go and just pray."

Of course, pray! Pray for guidance. And sooner or later, it always comes. But to hear it, you need to listen.

It was Ellie who taught me about Listening Prayer. She lent me a booklet, *Expectant Listening: Finding God's Thread of Guidance,* written by a Quaker, Michael Wajda, who explained it like this: "Many of us develop daily spiritual disciplines to seek God's guidance more fully. It is my experience that in seeking, we find. In listening, we hear God's messages. That is what I mean by 'expectant listening': Listening to hear God's messages."

Ellie said to do it any way you want. You can just sit quietly and lift your heart — maybe ask a question, maybe not — and then listen for that still, quiet voice. Sometimes Ellie hears it right away, sometimes later; but what amazes her is how often she hears it now that she's listening.

"It's funny," Ellie said. "All my life I'd been looking for someone who'd really listen and understand me, and all that time that someone was inside me. I don't know if it's God or me or my higher self. But you know what? It doesn't matter."

So I tried it, too, and sometimes I hear the answer clearly and feel touched by spirit. Other times, I hear nothing at all, yet still feel touched by spirit. Which reminds me of the Christian who told his pastor, "I pray and pray, but I don't get an answer." The pastor replied, "Your prayer *is* your answer. It's that very longing within you that connects you to the divine."

Reb Zalman taught me to talk to God. Ellie taught me to listen. But most of all what I've learned is this: Prayer is a way to *be* with God. It's the path I was searching for long ago, with a few million others who were looking for light.

BIRTH, MARRIAGE, AND DEATH

"So," Mom asked me, "are you done with your book?"

Almost, I said. Just a few things to cover.

"Like what?" Mom asked.

Like birth, marriage, and death.

She laughed, but I didn't.

Aargh! Three weighty topics. Too much to write. And that's why I kept putting it off.

Then I thought, Why not lump them together? I know, kind of cheap. But really, birth, marriage, and death are so sacred, what more can I say? Only this: Make each ritual truly yours.

When our friends Lori and Tom asked me to marry them (Colorado being one of those "whatever" states), I began to read up on weddings in different cultures. What I learned is this: They all follow a template, like a symphony in four movements. And it's that way, too, with ceremonies for baby naming or honoring the dead: Each has its own rhythm, purpose, and form, ripe with rituals that have lasted forever.

Rituals are like ladders: They can take you to a higher place. If you feel aligned with them, they will lend you their light, or you can alter them to make them your own. You do this by finding your way, your words, right from the heart. When that happens, a window opens, and everyone present is touched with grace.

I felt that grace at the naming ceremony for Brendan, our first grandchild, when friends and family sat around him and blessed him, one by one, with their wishes, while Cindy's Uncle John played on the piano a piece he had written in Brendan's honor.

I felt it, too, when John and I got married and the shaman who helped us write the ceremony had everyone present say together, "John and Rivvy, we now pronounce you husband and wife."

And I felt it at our friend Sara S.'s deathbed, when several of us gathered, lightly put our hands on her, and softly sang the lullaby "Angels watching over me, my Lord."

That same feeling was present at the funeral for Mom's late-in-life partner Len. After the burial, those closest to Len drove to his daughter Karen's house for lunch. At some point, the young rabbi asked us to form a circle with our chairs and then share, if we wished, stories about Len. Some of the stories made me laugh; some made me cry; and for the first time I thought, Now I know Len.

I felt grace again when Elise was in labor with Eli, her firstborn, and Joe, her husband, and I, her mom, stood by her bedside, counting through contractions and holding cool cloths on her forehead — even though she had initially claimed, "I might want my mom there, or I might want my husband there, but there's no way I can handle both of you at once!" I, too, had worried about how it would feel. But what I felt was grace.

I felt it once more when John's mum was dying and we flew to England to be with her. In the hospital by her bedside, I didn't know what to say. Then John started talking about the chocolate sponge pudding Mum made when he was young, and her summer frock with pink flowers … and that got her remembering, too, and saying, "We had some happy times, didn't we, dear?"

When we got home, after Mum died, we made an altar on our mantle, the way the Mexicans do on their Day of the Dead, and the way our friend Sarah does each year on the anniversary of her father's death. We placed Mum's picture in the center, along with roses, a candle, and chocolates, the kind she liked. Then we added ceramic miniatures of flowers, a lamb, and a watering can — things that felt like England and gardening and reminded us of Mum. And when we lit the candle, it all came alive, with an aura reflecting her spirit and life.

In truth, I feel grace at all weddings, births, and deaths. It's more than the words or the rituals; it's simply the essence of love.

So yes, Mom, the book is done.

Well, almost.

PICTURES AND WORDS

It was a time of slowness. John and I were building our house, or rather, beseeching the contractor to show up and get it built. And back in Philadelphia, my father was slowly dying. Each afternoon after work, I'd sit in the meadow in front of the slowly rising house, watch the sun go down, and think about Dad.

My dad and I never spoke much about feelings. In fact, we hardly spoke at all. He was from that generation of fathers who worked hard, came home for dinner, and let the mother do the talking. But I wanted to tell him before he died how much I loved him. I didn't know how much until he got sick. In my adolescence, we had a rough time, with lots of yelling and fights. I wasn't shy expressing my anger, and now I needed to express my love.

When I thought about that love, it came to me like this: how much fun he was and bursting with life ... the way he looked, so big and handsome ... how he'd bring us hot fudge sundaes and excitement when he came home from work ... his courage and irrepressible humor while facing a devastating disease....

I'll make him a book, I thought, a book of those moments. So I bought a small unlined journal and began to draw pictures and write simple prose, like a picture book for children.

"My father has big happy cheeks and warm brown eyes that twinkle," I wrote on page one. Then I drew a sketch of his happy, big-cheeked face.

"My dad is a teller of tales and a singer of songs. He played the ukulele and sang 'The Big Feet Blues': 'I've got the big feet blues, don't know what to dooz, Get up in the morning, can't put on my shoes.'"

"Summers with Dad: He took me to Phillies games, where we cheered and ate hot dogs with wonderful mustard ... On July 4th he grilled the best cheeseburgers I ever tasted and drove us to see the best fireworks ... And when I was really young, he played with me at the sea-shore and held me up to jump the waves."

On it went, memory after memory, page by page. Sometimes I cried while I wrote it, but it made me laugh, too, and it was working: The pictures and words were holding the love to honor him and say thanks.

My father, who rarely wrote or phoned me, sent me a letter when he received the book. He said he was "reading and rereading it" and that "reliving all the things we had done together" made him feel young. "I will cherish it forever," he wrote. "I love you very much."

He died seven months later. Now I read and reread his letter. I will cherish it forever. I love him very much.

Part Ten

THIS, TOO,
IS TRUE

*You can change in an instant —
and so can your life —
moment by moment by moment.*

JOY

"What are you writing?" my daughter asks, as we walk to the beach holding towels and pails and holding on to the hands of her two young sons.

"Little true stories," I say. "Recipes for a sacred life."

Elise gives me one of her knowing looks and gestures toward Eli and Isaac.

"You should write about your grandchildren," she says. "*They're* sacred."

SUMMER, 2009

In the glow of the setting sun, Eli, just four, and Isaac, almost two, race in circles on the dirt driveway by their farmhouse, while I vigorously chase them. Round and round we run, all laughing nonstop, as if this is the funniest thing in the world. And whenever I pause, gasping for breath, Isaac looks at me appealingly and says, "Maw! Maw!" Then we're off again, round and round, running and laughing.

Jenna Rose, at five-and-a-half, tosses her long hair — shiny and golden like her mother Cindy's — and asks if she can brush my shorter, darker tresses. She kneels behind me on the bed and brushes with long, slow strokes. "I'm making it grow longer," she says earnestly, and it feels so nice, as if my hair is truly growing with each stroke of the brush.

I'm sitting on the sofa reading *Mrs. Piggle-Wiggle,* a favorite book from my childhood, to Tony and Cindy's son, Brendan. Tall and lanky, he just turned seven, but still leans into my arms like a kitten when we read. He likes the book — "Not as much as *Harry Potter,*" he kindly explains, "but it's good too." He curls up happily and gently strokes my arm, and I feel the warmth of him and our love.

John walks over to the driveway to join the chasing game, pitching Eli and Isaac to a near-ecstatic state. Round and round we run, belly laughing, until loud honking sounds ripple above us, moving through the sky. "Geese!" Eli shouts. "Geeze!" Isaac shouts. And we all stop and gaze upward, like a moment of prayer.

There was a time in my life that seemed so painful I feared I was falling apart. So my mother came to New York to be with me and help me take care of my kids, her grandkids. "Hang in," she said. "Be strong. Because the good times will come back, I promise, and you want to be ready."

KINDNESS — RANDOM OR NOT

Many years ago a book came out called *Random Acts of Kindness,* and soon there were bumper stickers all over VWs imploring you to practice same. Next came a Random Kindness Website, a Random Kindness Foundation, and a Random Kindness Movement. But even with this overdose of random kindness (that no longer seemed that random), it always inspires me to hear stories about people who do something spontaneous, generous, and compassionate — without witnesses or acknowledgment.

One story I enjoyed was about a man who put extra coins in meters for cars parked near his own, especially those about to expire. I liked picturing people's faces when they came out to their car and saw they'd been saved by a mysterious stranger. I bet he liked picturing that too. But what made it extra nice was he didn't *need* to see them or be seen himself or thanked.

Sarah and I were talking on the phone about doing good things without talking about them and why that seems to be the higher way … but how some things you just *have* to tell. She then promptly told me one she had done, and we decided it was okay just telling me, as we often decide it's okay just me telling her.

Then she said that over the weekend her teen-age son, Dane, told her that he tries to do one random act of kindness each day.

"That's cool," Sarah told him, "like, what do you do?"

"Mom, I can't *tell* you," he said. "That would kind of negate it, you know?"

"Oh yeah," Sarah said. "But do you really do one a day?"

"I try to," Dane said.

"Like what?" Sarah asked.

"Mom!"

. . . .

> *"Be kind whenever possible.*
> *It is always possible."*
>
> — THE DALAI LAMA

SLOW

As time seems to move ever faster — and quantum physics suggests that it is — *we're* moving faster, too, and multitasking to keep up. But one July day in our warmest summer, the house was so hot I could barely move, and it was a challenge just to focus on *one* task. So I slowly emptied the dishwasher. Then I slowly cut flowers outside and arranged them in vases indoors. And when my mother called that evening, I listened to her without simultaneously checking my email.

What I realized was this: When I slow down, I feel truly connected with the task or object or person at hand.

Connected with the peacock-patterned dishes from Czechoslovakia that I took out of the dishwasher and put away, while remembering my nana who had passed them down. Connected with the orange, pink, and coral zinnias I cut, while noticing how each color set off the other in a soft yet vibrant way. Connected to my mother, to what she was saying and the feelings beneath.

Once again I was reminded that connection is the path to sacred living, and doing one thing at a time — slowly — is one way there.

THE SOUNDS OF MUSIC

In my twenties, when I vowed to live *intensely* and experience *everything*, I spent most of my weekends at the movies. On Saturdays, there were double features, and I once sat through three films by Jean-Luc Godard (or maybe I just saw *Breathless* three times).

What gave movies an edge over life? The soundtrack. I imagined how much better life would be if it only had a soundtrack. Even the hard parts could be softened with a few violins.

The universe was clearly attuned to my thoughts, for some years later the iPod was born. Till then, we settled for stereo. I remember when stereo first came out and a friend taught me how to find the best spot in the room to get its full effect. If I needed more proof of music's magic, that was it: There was one spot where it all came together just right.

Music is like prayer: I forget how powerful it is and how quickly it can lift me. The highest I ever went was in Venice, Italy, with John. In a small, golden-lit chapel, a group of inspired musicians played Vivaldi concertos as we sat and listened in awe. Or maybe it was walking into a rock concert in Rye, New York, just as Janis Joplin was belting out "Piece of My Heart" — with such power and passion I can still hear it.

Another gift of music is its synergy: It can make anything feel more sacred and fun — cooking, eating, or making love. And while it often brings me into the moment, it can also pull me back to the past. Listening to "oldies but goodies" or folk songs from the '60s, I relive first love: the pleasure, the pain; marriage and babies; dreams and loss ... and I get to see the movie that's the movie of my life.

So of course I bought an iPod.

My kids were impressed, knowing my discomfort with anything high-tech. They were less impressed when I kept it in its box for two years, along with the digital camera and other gadgets I seem unable to comprehend. Then Joe, our son-in-law, came to visit, connected the iPod to my computer, and taught me how to upload and download.

The weekend Joe left, I sat in my office and filled the iPod with every CD we owned: Sly and the Family Stone, Bach's Brandenburg concertos, West African drumming, The Beatles .... Soon I was rocking in my chair to Paul Simon singing "Graceland." I grew misty hearing Andrea Bocelli's *Romanza*. And when the theme from *Evita* came on — "Don't Cry for Me, Argentina" — I was crying too.

Higher and higher I went as I played Mozart ... Dylan ... John Denver ... Aretha ... and Mexican music that made me get up and dance. Ray Charles was next, singing the blues, and stamp-your-feet gospel took me straight to God, I swear it.

I spent that whole day alone in my office, uploading, downloading, crying, and dancing. And when I went downstairs to make a pie, I turned up the speakers in the kitchen and living room, plugged in the iPod, and clicked on a medley Paul H. had made for us: Joan Baez, Pete Seeger, and, as a bonus, Louis Armstrong. Louis was singing "What a Wonderful World." It felt as achingly sweet as love.

When John came home, he heard the music from upstairs, downstairs, and all around us and said, "You've got music everywhere." Which is what I always wanted, a soundtrack for my life.

· · · · · · · · ·

*"Music washes away from the soul
the dust of everyday life."*
— NED ROREM

FORTUNE COOKIE KARMA

Jeanne and I walked to the Pearl Street Mall and had dinner at a new Asian restaurant — very hip, very Thai, very Boulder. But when the waitress brought the bill, she gave us the same old fortune cookies from the Chinese restaurants of my youth in Philly. The fortunes, however, were on a whole new level. Instead of "You will be rich and famous and travel to many countries," I got:

> *"Doing the best at this moment puts you in the best place for the next moment."*

Whoa! I immediately switched my focus more onto what Jeanne was saying and less on my travails, which I was waiting to tell her.

It was a karma wake-up call, and a hopeful one at that. You can change in an instant — and so can your life — moment by moment by moment.

DO A *MITZVAH*.
WHAT'S A *MITZVAH*?

When I was young, I didn't know what a *mitzvah* was. I only knew from the way my mother said it that it was something big.

"Aunt Sally is sick again," I'd say. "I guess I should go see her. But it's snowing and I have a report to finish and Aunt Sally's always grumpy...."

"See her," my mom would interrupt and then add with enthusiasm, "It's a *mitzvah!*"

She made a *mitzvah* sound special, even jolly. Visiting Aunt Sally?

I now know that *mitzvah,* a Hebrew word, has many meanings. First off, it means "commandment, divine law, or the fulfillment of same." But it also means "connection" and has come to mean "a blessing." How does a commandment become a connection and blessing? It works like this:

While we are always connected to our divine source or higher self, it's when we follow the divine laws that we get to feel and express that connection. Spirit asks, we respond, and our lives become blessed.

There is no lack of opportunities to feel this connection since the Torah is chock-full of commandments. Along with the Big Ten — *Thou shall not steal* et al — there are 603 others. Some tell you what to do: *Leave a corner of the field uncut for the poor. Return a lost object.* Others tell what not to do: *Don't hurt orphans. Don't bear a grudge.* And they refer to all aspects of life since all of life can be made holy. It's even a *mitzvah* to make love with your mate.

But over the years, *mitzvah* has come to mean simply a good deed, *any* good deed. And doing *mitzvot* is considered the way to live a good life and find happiness.

The idea that good deeds may be the path to happiness is not just a religious concept, but might be ingrained in our DNA. Scientists have discovered that altruistic actions often lead to a happier, healthier life. One study even shows that giving to charity affects the same part of our brain that is stimulated by sex, drugs, and money (which sounds like the lead-in to a Woody Allen joke: "So this guy says to me, 'Hey, Mister, you got a dollar?'").

Now, for many years, I didn't know these laws or studies, but I always knew when I was doing a good deed, and that always felt great. And when you do a *mitzvah,* you not only feel blessed, but *are* blessed — often watched over and guided. That's what happened to me when my father died.

My sisters, who live in California, and John and I in Boulder immediately made plans to fly to Philadelphia for the funeral. Still, there would be a few days before then when our mother would be alone, and I was the only one who was able to go right away. I was also the only one who, at that time, suffered anxiety attacks if flying solo. But thinking of Mom all alone made me book the ticket.

I packed my security items — prayer beads, spiritual books, and a cheesy love novel — kissed John goodbye, and walked with fear into the plane. Once seated, I began to pray: *Please God, don't let me have an anxiety attack, let me be okay.* Then I looked around and saw that the plane was half empty. So once everyone settled in, I decided to change my seat. Row 9, my lucky number, was totally free. I first tried 9E, but then moved to 9A, a window seat that seemed to draw me to it. I buckled up and said a silent prayer of thanks for having the whole row to myself.

Just then, amid announcements of takeoff, a late-comer, looking upset and disheveled, burst in. He viewed his ticket to find his seat and sat down right next to me. With all these empty seats, he had to have 9B? Why did I leave 9E? I opened my cheesy novel to read, hoping he'd leave me alone.

But that was not to be. He was clearly geared up and started to talk. "Good book?" he asked. "Supposedly," I answered, a little embarrassed to be reading it in the first place. "*The Bridges of Madison County,*" he said, viewing the title. "Is it about bridges?" "No," I said, more embarrassed still, "it's about love." Sensing his need to talk, I put the book down and looked at him more closely.

His face was unshaven, his clothes were rumpled, and he was holding a tattered brown notebook. Its title was penciled in: "Job's Journal." He's looking for work, I thought, and hasn't had much schooling. He doesn't know it should be "Job Journal."

"Are you looking for a job?" I asked, nodding at his notebook.

"No," he said, and smiled wanly. "I changed my name to Job, after Job in the Bible. You know, the one who suffered more than any man should bear."

Then he told me his own story and I understood why.

Like Job, he had been stricken with loss, one after the other. But unlike Job, a man of faith and integrity, his had been self-inflicted — through ego, betrayals, and lies. Once a youthful idealist, he was now, he acknowledged, notorious and loathed. He had lost everything — most of all, his character — and despite his efforts to redeem himself, he felt beyond redemption because his actions had destroyed the lives of others. Still, I sensed hope in his present endeavor: as a clown who entertained children in hospitals.

The plane was lifting into the sky now, and I felt my hands begin to sweat. But my fellow passenger was compelling, and we continued to talk.

It was when I told him about my dad that I suddenly noticed and remarked, "Your eyes are so much like his, it's strange." Dark-brown slanty eyes, with the same twinkle, sadness, and depth.

"What's your name?" he asked and then told me his, "Matusow. Job Matusow."

"Matusow?" I repeated. "That was my dad's mother's name, Helen Matusow."

We soon discovered we were cousins, distant cousins who had never met.

Job looked at me with my father's eyes and said softly, "Your dad is still with you." And I knew it was true.

Which is why when Aunt Sally calls, sick and grumpy, and it's snowing outside and I have work to do, I go and see her. How could I not? It's a *mitzvah*.

A WAY TO DANCE

A funny thing about the spiritual is how often it's physical. It's not about leaving your body but being fully in it. Then, with a little help from grace, your energy merges with the energy around you, and you are fully present, fully alive.

For me, this alchemy happens when I deeply engage in the following:

Walking, simply walking, and seeing things I never see from a car.

Free dancing with the music, myself, and the room — and the sky as well, coming in through the window.

Making love, making love, making love!

Circle dancing with the Sufis, swaying, whirling, and chanting, chanting the names of God.

Hiking on trails where I feel myself guided as I look for each marker painted on trees, and follow that path through forests and glades until reaching the place where I first began.

Dancing the hora at Jewish weddings, all holding hands in a swirling circle as the klezmer music gets louder and faster and the bride and groom are raised high on chairs.

Bicycling down country roads, passing farms and wild roses, as I watch the world go by like a movie.

Doing yoga, especially outdoors, when the birds are singing, a breeze is blowing, and it becomes, more than ever, meditation in motion.

Square dancing so fast I can feel my heart beating, and my cheeks get red and hurt from smiling. Faster and stamping, doing the reel, so everyone dances with everyone else. Bow to your partner, bow to your corner, a way to honor each person you pass.

In each of these, I feel the ecstasy of being. And each of them is a way to dance.

. . . .

"To dance then, is to pray, to meditate,
to enter into communion with the larger dance,
which is the universe."

— JEAN HOUSTON

TIKKUN OLAM

When our country was at war in Vietnam, there was
march after march in a movement for peace. Each time,
it seemed, more people came marching — parents and
children; students and workers; hippies, seniors, and
nuns. The last march I went to, in Washington, had a
crowd that stretched farther than you could see, and our
hope was rising along with our numbers.

In May of the year when that war finally ended, a
celebration took place in Central Park. Joan Baez was
there, and so were countless others. It was a communal
explosion of sorrow and joy, and there was comfort in
knowing we each played our small part.

But years later, when our country was more secretly
involved in a civil war in El Salvador, I found myself
marching again. This time the rally was at Columbia
University on a cold winter day, and there were fewer than
eighty of us there. I didn't know anyone, and most people
were much younger than myself. Instead of feeling communal, I felt out of place, and wished I'd stayed home
where it was cozy and warm. Then they started chanting:

"What do we want? Peace! When do we want it? Now!"

The same words we had chanted so many years before
at so many marches. A shiver went through me; I was back
where I belonged. At the same time, it felt sad and ironic
to hear the same old chants and wonder when, if ever, war
would end.

The rally leaders directed us toward the streets, and an older man holding a peace sign passed beside me. He was a well-known New York activist, and we had met at rallies before.

"Here we go again," I said, smiling but discouraged. "How much longer do we need to do this?"

His answer was simple: "Until there's no more war."

In Kabbalah lore, there's a myth of creation. When God first made the world, it says, he poured divine light into clay vessels to make every-thing shine with holiness. But the vessels were fragile and they shattered, trapping sparks of light beneath pieces of clay.

Some say that's why God made people: to find and free the holy light. Others say God always meant to leave the world imperfect so we could work with him, as partners, to perfect it.

Isaac Luria, a 16th century mystic, first told this myth. He said it explained our collective task: *tikkun olam,* a Hebrew term that means "to heal or repair the world." In Jewish tradition, this can mean working for peace and justice, or protecting the environment, or doing what-ever we can to spread the light.

Where to begin?

Wherever you're drawn. The world has no lack of problems.

What can we do?

There's something for everyone. Even signing a petition can make a difference and let you feel the power of community.

How long do we need to do this?

Until the world is healed.

Tikkun olam.

SPEAKING SPANISH IN MEXICO

I was going to list the things I do that make my life feel sacred, things like painting, tutoring, and playing the guitar. Or watching the moonrise and speaking Spanish in Mexico. Things that lift me out of my self, into connection, and often into a state of joy.

Then I realized that this would be *my* list, and what makes them sacred is doing things that I love. So your list might be, well, whatever connects you with your passion and love. And when you do what you love, you feel love. It's that simple.

. . . .

Let the beauty we love be what we do.
There are hundreds of ways to kiss the ground.

— RUMI

FOR DAYS WHEN IT'S HARD
TO FEEL GRATEFUL

So there I was practicing gratefulness, and on good days, no problem. "Oh thank you for this lovely sky. And my dear family. And thank you for my loving husband, John." Then, when the dark days came, I would struggle to feel gratitude but find it forced and phony. I'd be praying, "Thank you, God, I'm really grateful for this lesson ... or challenge ... or, um, chance to grow ..." — but I wasn't. What I wanted to say was "Help! Make things better! This is so not okay!"

Then I found a little book by Richard Carlson: *Don't Sweat the Small Stuff ... and it's all small stuff.* He wrote that the happiest people he knew were hardly happy all the time. *That's encouraging.* In fact, they could really get down. *All right!* The key seemed to be their awareness that bad times and bad moods will come. So rather than fight them, they just accept them, and wait for them to pass. *Yeah, but bad times can get worse and drag on and* — And they pass a lot quicker, Carlson added, if you accept them with grace.

Ah, now I got it. It was like finding the missing piece of a puzzle. Good day, be grateful. Bad day, be graceful. Be grateful, be graceful, and on it goes.

ONE LAST SONG

My mother, Irene Feldman, is a singer. She once audi-
tioned in New York for Irving Berlin, who offered her
a gig that very night. But she was young and scared and
went back to Philly — to be a housewife, raise three kids,
and star in such synagogue specials as *Porgy and Bess*. Two
of those kids, sister Susan and I, shared her aspirations,
which we displayed at an early age by singing show tunes
at dinner. Susan went on to make it to Broadway. I just
went on. But I went on singing, a way to open my heart.

It wasn't until I moved to Boulder that I first
attended a singing party. Helen and Allan often had
them at their house in the mountains. They would make
copies of the songs for that evening, though anyone
could start a song they liked. One night, near the winter
solstice, I went there with Paul and Jeanne, even though I
had the winter blues and was *not* in the mood for singing
(in fact, I was thinking, Oh Puleez!). But I *was* in the
mood for drinking. So once we arrived, I poured a glass
of Bailey's, sat near the fire, and listened.

Some of the people sang solos, which were pleasant
to hear; but mostly we sang together, which raised the
room's energy much more. It felt good to be with people
and not have to talk — just everyone together, singing.
Especially rousing were old-time favorites ("She'll
be Comin' 'Round the Mountain"), gospel music
("Amazing Grace"), and top hits from *My Fair Lady*.

When we bundled up to leave, Helen told me, "I'm glad you came. I could tell you were a little sad at first. The singing did you good." And as we drove down the mountain, Jeanne said, "Singing is healing." I nodded and thought of my mom.

When my mother was eighty-eight, she entered the hospital for a second go at experimental heart surgery that had almost killed her the first time. Her three daughters — Susan, Judy, and I — all flew in to be there. As Mom waited to be taken to the operating room, we sat together on her bed; and though she looked small and frail in her hospital gown, she seemed strong in spirit. Stronger than *I* felt, for sure. I was scared and didn't know what to say to her in those pre-op moments. After all, the doctors had been clear: It was a gamble; she could die.

I wanted to say something meaningful, words that were worthy of maybe being my last, but still sound up-beat and reassuring. An impossible task. So instead of talking, I started to sing — a takeoff of "Frère Jacques" — and my sisters soon joined in:

> *"Reenie Feldman, Reenie Feldman,*
> *We love you,*
> *Yes we do,*
> *You're our dearest mother,*
> *There could be no other,*
> *One like you,*
> *We love you."*

Mom loved it. So much so that when we finished, she sang to us. It was a song she had performed at age five at a movie theater talent show: "Me Without You," a Betty Boop kind of ditty. She followed up with a lively Yiddish love song, *"Sheyn Vi Di Levuneh"* (You're as beautiful as the moon). Susan caught it all on her BlackBerry, and then an intern came to take Mom away. As he wheeled her out on the gurney, headed for surgery, she blew us kisses until out of sight.

This time, the operation worked. But Lord, had it failed, what a good day to die.

Right, Mom said, but what a great day to live.

ACKNOWLEDGMENTS

If I ever won an Academy Award, they'd have to drag me off the stage. That said, here goes:

Deepest thanks to my first readers for their encouragement, faith, and invaluable feedback: Sarah Bowler, Barbara Fisher, Helen Turner, John Wilcockson, and Irene Feldman. Lasting gratitude to my wise and wonderful agent, Kristina Holmes, whose strategic powers allowed her to tame the force of Mercury in retrograde to find us our made-in-heaven publisher, Divine Arts.

I am ever grateful to Michael Wiese and Geraldine Overton-Wiese for having the heart, vision, and wisdom to create Divine Arts, and for giving me such a loving welcome and support. To them and to all the Divine Arts team — especially Manny Otto and Travis Masch, who helped in every way; John Brenner and Jay Anning, who made it all look so wonderful; and Matt Barber, my kind and keen-eyed copy editor — I thank you with all my heart for believing in my book and helping it to be born into the world.

With great appreciation for those who guided me through this mysterious process: Hal Zinna Bennett, Jim Levine, Jenny Bent, and the many members of Boulder Media Women for their encouragement and advice. And loving thanks to all who lent a hand along the way: Angela Bowman, Laura Marshall, Judy Feldman, Mary

Benjamin, Bella Stander, Paul and Jeanne Visvader, Susan Feldman, Martha Griffin, Emily Spielman, Jody Berman, Lisa Trank Greene, Karen Wegela, Paul Hansen, Elise Berkman, Cindy Berkman, Roslyn Schloss, Danielle Poitras, Susan Rose, Celia Bockhoff, and Zach and Kimmerjae Johnson.

I felt blessed by those who endorsed this book early on: Rabbi Zalman Schachter-Shalomi, Marilyn Webb, Barbara Fisher, Ally Sheedy, Hal Zinna Bennett, Jay Neugeboren, Priscilla Stuckey, and Bryan Luke Seaward. And special thanks are offered to Byrd Baylor and Peter Parnell for their inspiring book *The Way to Start the Day*; to Uncle Greg, Aunt Emma, and Uncle Bob, for their inspiration as good writers and good people; and to all the photographers whose pictures grace these pages: Jack Greene, Barry Berkman, Iván Loire, Stanley Lanzano, Mula Eshet, and Mary Frances Carmell.

I gratefully acknowledge my teachers who are featured in these stories: family and friends, neighbors and strangers, and all other seekers and messengers of truth.

Yes, yes, I know, time to end. So lastly, but most resoundingly, my thanks go to John, for everything. And I bow with gratitude to the Divine Spirit, from where these stories most magically came, and to you, dear reader, for whom they were meant.

ENDNOTES AND PERMISSIONS

I am grateful to the following for their inspiration and, where needed, reprint permissions.

Beginnings: The "Find Your Highest Purpose" quiz was inspired by Marcia Wieder in her book *Making Your Dreams Come True*, Harmony Books, New York: 1999.

Part 1: Basic Ingredients: *Photo Courtesy of U.S. Army.*

The Where to Begin: Recipe inspired by Deepak Chopra in his book *The Seven Spiritual Laws of Success*, Amber-Allen Publishing and New World Library, California: 1994

Grateful in Harlem: Ending quotation from *Start Where You Are*, by Pema Chödrön, ©1994 by Pema Chödrön. Reprinted by arrangement with Shambhala Publications Inc., Boston, MA. www.shambhala.com.

Miracles to Share: Quotes from *Stand like Mountain, Flow like Water,* by Brian Luke Seaward (HCI, Deerfield Beach, Florida: 1997), are reprinted courtesy of author.

This too shall pass: Quotes from Claudia Dreifus's interview with the Dalai Lama, *AARP The Magazine*, March 2006. Copyright, Claudia Dreifus. Reprinted by permission.

Part 2: The Sun Is Rising: *Photo courtesy of Iván Loire, www.2earth.org.*

Hello to the Sun: Verse from *The Way to Start a Day*, written by Byrd Baylor and illustrated by Peter Parnall, Aladdin Books, New York: 1978. Text copyright, Byrd Baylor. Reprinted by permission of author.

The First Few Steps: My morning prayer was inspired by Victor Villaseñor's *Rain of Gold,* A Delta Book, Dell Publishing, New York: 1991.

The gatha "Waking Up" is reprinted from *Present Moment Wonderful Moment: Mindfulness Verses for Daily Living* (1990) by Thich Nhat Hanh with permission of Parallax Press, Berkeley, California, www.parallax.org.

Part 3: Animal Chats and Other Unions with Nature: *Photo: Copyright © Mula Eshet/Robert Harding World Imagery/Corbis, reprinted by permission.*

Part 4: To Forgive Is Divine: *Photo courtesy of Stanley Lanzano, from his book:* True Places: A Lowcountry Preacher, His Church and His People.

What the Dalai Lama Said: "Forgiveness interventions" were reported in Melissa Healy's article "Forgive and be well?", The Los Angeles Times, December 31, 2007.

Rites of forgiveness: The forgiveness exercise described is from Shakti Gawain's book *Creative Visualization.* Copyright © 2002 by Shakti Gawain. Reprinted with permission of New World Library, Novato, CA. www.newworldlibrary.com.

Part 5: Friends and Neighbors ...: *Photo courtesy of Jack Greene, www.rosewentlovely.com.*

Do You Give to the Ones Who Are Drunk? Rabbi, philosopher, and physician Moses Maimonides' writings on "tzedakah" are found in the Mishneh Torah, chapter 10.

Have a great day! ...: Lines from "Textures," courtesy of poet Stan Grotegut.

Studies correlating gratitude with well-being include one by R.A. Emmons and M.E. McCullough: "Counting blessings versus burdens: An experimental investigation of gratitude and subjective well-being in daily life," *Journal of Personality and Social Psychology, 84*(2), 377-389. (2003)

Take Care of Each Other: Lyrics from "Let There Be Love," written by Ian Grant and Lionel Rand. Used by Permission of Shapiro, Bernstein & Co., Inc. All Rights Reserved. International Copyright Secured.

Part 6: A Nature Recipe ...: *Photo courtesy of Jack Greene, www.rosewentlovely.com.*

Part 7: Sacred Space ...: *Photo courtesy of Jack Greene, www.rosewentlovely. com*

Quote from a conversation with Brian Spielmann, by his permission.

Zen View: The "Zen View" concept is from *A Pattern Language: Towns · Buildings · Construction*, by Christopher Alexander, Sara Ishikawa, and Murray Silverstein, of the Center for Environmental Structure, with Max Jacobson, Ingrid Fiksdahl-King, and Shlomo Angel. Oxford University Press, USA: 1977.

Part 8: Soul Food: *Family photo of Passover Seder, circa 1954. Rivvy sits on the right behind her father and sister Susan and across from her mother and sister Judy.*

Part 9: Rituals and Celebrations ...: *Photo of Tony and Cindy Berkman, courtesy of Mary Frances Carmell.*

Looking for Light: Quotation from Michael Wajda's *Expectant Listening: Finding God's Thread of Guidance*, Pendle Hill Pamphlet #388 (Wallingford, Pennsylvania: Pendle Hill Publications, 2007), p. 4. Permission granted.

Part 10: This, Too, Is True: *Photo of Eli and Isaac Lipman, courtesy of their grandfather Barry Berkman.*

Do a *Mitzvah*. **What's a** *Mitzvah*? Researchers at the National Institutes of Health discovered that giving affects the same part of the brain stimulated by sex, drugs and money (Robert Franklin, *Minneapolis–St. Paul Star Tribune*, February 21, 2007).

For Days When It's Hard to Feel Grateful: Story inspired by Dr. Richard Carlson in his book *Don't Sweat the Small Stuff ... and it's all small stuff*, Hyperion, New York: 1997.

Author's photo by Darcy Kiefel, *www.kiefelphotography.com*.

ABOUT THE AUTHOR

Darcy Kiefel, kiefelphotography.com

Rivvy Neshama is a writer, editor, and community organizer whose spiritual path draws from many sources: Eastern and Western religions, Native traditions, Sufis and shamans, and her mom. Along the way, she earned a bachelor's degree in philosophy from Bryn Mawr College and master's degrees in comparative literature, social work, and education.

Rivvy has been a teacher and social worker in Harlem, a college instructor in Queens, and a Tarot card reader at Macy's on Halloween. She was the founding development director of *Intercambio* — Uniting Communities, in Colorado. And as a co-founder and first director of Transportation Alternatives, the advocacy group for bicycling, walking, and public transit in New York City, she was profiled in *Ms.* magazine.

A lifelong writer, Rivvy was first published in *Story* magazine's best college writing anthology, and has since written for many national publications, including *Ms.*, *Glamour*, and *The New York Times*. She is the author of the children's book *Nat Turner and the Virginia Slave Revolt*.

Rivvy lives in Boulder, Colorado, and Sag Harbor, New York, with her husband, British author John Wilcockson.

www.rivvyneshama.com